No Particular Place to Go: The Making of a Free High School

by Steve Bhaerman
and Joel Denker

SIMON AND SCHUSTER : NEW YORK

FIRST PRINTING

SBN 671–21146–3
Library of Congress Catalog Card Number: 77–179581
Designed by Irving Perkins
Manufactured in the United States of America
By H. Wolff Book Mfg. Co., Inc., New York, N.Y.

To the kids of the New Educational Project,
classes of '69 and '70.

ACKNOWLEDGMENTS

Without the friendship and support of all the people in the New Educational Project this book would not have been possible. We want especially to thank Kathy, Greg, Norm, Matt, and Carol. We are indebted to two close friends, Paul Lauter and Florence Howe, who helped to inspire many of our ideas on education. We are grateful to our editor, Dan Green. Flo Bergin heroically typed our many manuscripts. Ronald Gross and Paul Osterman encouraged us to write this book. Our parents encouraged us while it was being born. Many friends kept us sane while we were writing it: in Staten Island, Tuck and Mary, John and Sue, Jim and John; in Coburn, Cyndee, Wyatt, Sean, Robin, Susie, Garvin, Mike, Judy, the Ferns, the Broskleys, the Schaffers; in Washington, Carol and Charles, Stan Sloss and the Fessenden Street commune, Roger and Norma.

Contents

Foreword

Public high schools in suburbia are exploding. In the last few years boycotts, sit-ins, and other acts of rebellion have shattered these outwardly placid communities. Militant protests, though, are only the most visible sign of the disaffection that many white middle-class kids feel. All over the country small groups of students are banding together to form free schools. They are doing this with the help of discontented teachers, parents, and other friendly souls.

But it is their boldness more than anything else that supplies the real energy for these projects. For dropping out of school means not only overcoming the resistance of one's parents but also confronting the many regulations that restrict the freedom of the young—the compulsory attendance, labor, antiloitering, and other laws.

In 1968 the two of us, both then teachers in public high schools, helped a group of Washington area students to create an alternative to schools they found boring and oppressive. The free school, the New Educational Project, was distinctive in a number of ways. We were working with white middle-class kids when many progressive white teachers our age were teaching in ghetto schools in Washington. We also built our project on the foundation of communal living. At least half of the kids and most of the adults lived in houses we rented in Washington and suburban Maryland.

This book is both the story of the school during 1968–70 and a record of how our lives were shaped by our involvement in it. In our narrative we try to unite the personal and the abstract. We want to show how our changes in consciousness—

9

our concepts of learning, of community, of politics—had their roots in the practical experiences of communal living, of running a project. Our book will illustrate the constant conflict between our rhetoric, our expectations, and the tangled reality we discovered as we built the school.

Since our perspectives on the school were different, though complementary, each of us has written separate chapters. We write in the first person in order to enhance the intensity and uniqueness of our experiences.

If readers wish to correspond with us about our project or about free schools in general, they may write to us in care of Simon and Schuster, 630 Fifth Ave., New York, N.Y. 10020.

CHAPTER I

Steve: A Personal
Introduction

1. *Growing Up in Brooklyn*

Unlike most of the people I worked with at the free school, my parents were working class, the children of Jewish, eastern European immigrants. Both had an ingrained respect for education and a desire to transcend the working class, yet neither was able to attend college. My father got as far as the eighth grade before he left school to work. My mother was an excellent student who had the misfortune to be a teen-ager during the Depression. She, too, was forced to give up her education in order to help support her family.

I inherited much of my alienation from my parents. Both were fervent New Dealers who felt very much out of place during the Eisenhower era. FDR had been their hero—he successfully waged war against the Depression and the Nazis. But Roosevelt was dead, and they felt especially bitter and cynical about contemporary politics. The Depression shattered their belief in the American Dream.

Even in the prosperous postwar period they felt uneasy; fear of future depressions had made them overly cautious and security-conscious. They were embittered by the anti-Semitism of the thirties—they vividly remembered the America Firsters,

Father Coughlin, the well-attended Bund rallies. When my mother applied for a job with the Metropolitan Life Insurance Company during the Depression and came to the question "Which church do you attend?" she knew she had no chance.

At an early age I understood and accepted my parents' resentment of the "business world." My father had always worked for someone else, usually someone who took advantage of him. When he worked in the fur trade he remained loyal to his boss even in the face of possible beatings by goons. He had seen too much cruelty on the part of union organizers to be radical. During the early thirties, when he first began to work, he saw Communist organizers cripple the hands of old craftsmen who refused to join the union. Despite his loyalty, when work in the industry got slow, he was laid off. An old boss offered him a job in a hotel. He spent the next ten years working at the hotel between serious illnesses. His last stint was in the "package room," a damp alcove in the hotel's cellar. He left for work at 5:30 A.M. and frequently worked six days a week. Finally, in 1964, illness forced him to quit for good.

For many the postwar period was a time of mobility. Soldiers returning home married, went to college, took new jobs and found new roots. Millions left the familiar ethnic neighborhood for the modern, faceless suburbs, left their working-class backgrounds behind for white-collar jobs. For the first few years of my life I was raised in an extended family. Aunts, uncles, cousins, grandparents all lived within a few blocks of one another. But America beckoned and all but a few left.

My parents were too old, too afraid, to make such a move. They were too busy with daily survival to become very much involved with the consumer rat race. During that time they felt bitter and frustrated that they couldn't live in a better neighborhood, that they couldn't provide their children with more material comfort. Yet as a result of their "deprivation," they managed to maintain a degree of integrity and perspective. Because they had had little need to maintain a middle-class façade, because they have had so little to defend, they have come to realize that they haven't missed much at all—that

America is an empty seduction that offers no roots, no love, no spirit, only insatiability. My parents, who left the old neighborhood belatedly, who stayed a little too long at the housing project, who didn't adopt the pretensions of our more middle-class relatives, may have had the last laugh.

When we did leave the old neighborhood, we moved to a predominately black housing project in Bedford-Stuyvesant (the black ghetto in Brooklyn). More than ever we had to re-affirm our roots in order to survive the dead-end negativity of the ghetto. Despite their distaste for organized religion, my parents clung to Jewish values and traditions: a respect for education, hard work, cleanliness, and sobriety. Because my parents embraced these middle-class values, I often felt alienated from the housing-project culture. I felt oppressed by its violence and squalor, resented and hated the black kids who did not conform to my standards of "civilized behavior." In school I stood out as "smart," as "different." I was the symbolic Jew in a black Babylon, proclaiming an alien culture. I learned to expect and accept aggression, to keep my hatred to myself. I was re-enacting the Jewish drama—suffering because I was "superior."

When other kids accepted aggression as a matter of course, I could never shrug it off. My father often spoke of his exploits in ethnic gang wars, and I wanted desperately to live up to his image. I stubbornly and foolishly resisted bullies, even when I knew I would be beaten up, because I carried this Jewish burden on my shoulders. The more I got beaten up, the more "special" I felt. Frequently my manner itself was enough to provoke fights. In class I refused to let other kids copy answers from me. I found schoolwork easy and had little compassion for classmates who had more trouble. I felt that I was "earning my own way" and that they should do likewise.

Yet I was hardly a goody-goody. I was a noisy, restless child who hated being cooped up or shut up. School deepened my conflicts because it reinforced the accepted mode of behavior—docility and studiousness. I wanted to excel in school, but I wanted to be part of my father's world too. The school made me feel the two were incompatible. I had no model to look up to—I didn't have a male teacher until the seventh grade. In danger of winning the fifth-grade spelling bee, I purposely misspelled an easy word to avoid the embarrassment of being good at "girls' stuff."

When I reached junior high school I was placed in a "special progress class," an accelerated group that enabled me to skip the eighth grade. More important, I was finally with a peer group that stimulated me to be myself. I no longer felt defensive about my intellectual abilities, nor did I feel the need to play the role of "smart kid." I felt somewhat relieved not to be at the top of my class, glad that I was not the focus of attention.

As I began to feel more relaxed with my new schoolmates I felt less of a need to prove myself to the project kids, less of a need to suffer. Because I accepted myself more, the neighborhood kids came to accept me too. Mostly we respected our differences. Since I was "intellectual," no one expected me to become involved in the local gang wars. My aloofness was my protection. A local kid whom I hardly knew would sometimes shout hello to me to indicate to his friends that I was "all right."

If I felt uncomfortable as the only white in a black neighborhood, I felt equally uncomfortable with the white middle-class kids I encountered in high school. They were wealthier, more poised than my friends from junior high school. I did make some new friends, but our friendship ended abruptly when school was out. I never dreamed of asking anyone to my house. Even my junior high school friends were afraid to come to the "project."

During high school I avoided dating (which is not to say that I had much actual avoiding to do—few girls considered me a desirable date). I was suspicious of most relationships because I felt that love was exploitative anyway, that sex was a commodity. I learned that you competed for love objects the way you competed for anything else—by using your position and your possessions as weapons. Coming from the housing project, I didn't have much of an arsenal.

More sophisticated friends spoke of making an investment in

a girl: after a certain number of expensive dates the stock paid off. I had neither the means nor the desire to involve myself in this sort of economic relationship. Instead, I stayed around my old friends, mostly fantasizing about the girls we knew. Together we reinforced our frustration. In school we were "strangers" who drifted along from class to class without submitting any more than we had to. At three o'clock we came strangely alive. None of us lingered in school any longer than we had to. I was proud to have no student activities listed next to my name in the high school yearbook. Even then I believed that extracurricular activities—dances and basketball games— were nothing but lollipops to make the rest of the tiresome bullshit more acceptable.

As an outsider, I had a solid perspective on the destructiveness of high school life. However, I could find no way to express myself. I was rootless; I felt part of no group, I could find little to identify with in American culture. Rock music was raunchy and rebellious but did not have the same cultural significance as it has had in the past few years. It expressed a vague unrest, yet the lyrics rarely dealt with complex feelings. Although I enjoyed listening to it, I could never identify with the soppy, stereotyped themes of most songs.

During my early teens I faithfully read *Mad* magazine, which reinforced my cynicism and dislike of Madison Avenue. I suppose if I had heard of Lenny Bruce at the time, I would have embraced his type of urban iconoclasm. Profanity seemed to be the most accurate way to describe America of the fifties. My secret hero was Holden Caulfield's compatriot, who graphically expressed his frustration by farting in church.

I never identified much with the Beats; to me they seemed weak and self-indulgent. Convinced that they could change nothing, they retreated into their world of jazz, poetry, and drugs. I suppose I might have been better off had I focused my energy on music or writing. But I avoided the bohemian kids because I still felt insecure about my intellectual image; I was still trying to impress an imaginary peer group. I tried to throw off the stigma of being different by acting like everyone else.

At fifteen I bought a set of barbells to build myself up. In junior high school I became a fanatic baseball fan—I kept elaborate records of all the major-league players. Slowly this became my world. I retreated into the lives and records of my heroes. I became the "record keeper," sort of a god over my little universe. Every year there would be a new crop of rookies and a few veterans would retire. As the recorder of events, I would remain unchanged, immortal. I found this role much less threatening than real involvement would have been.

Only once did I examine my rather strange life. One night, shortly after I was sixteen, I became caught up with the idea of death. This was scary enough, but I soon began to think beyond death, of infinity. I could not shut out the thought of a deep, abysmal infinity on all sides of me. For days I could hardly eat or function normally. As I watched people going through their mundane nine-to-five lives I wondered how they could concern themselves with such trivia in the face of eventual death.

This wasn't a great religious experience for me—I could see nothing beyond the world of human contrivances. I decided that the things people did each day were the actual substance of life. I found little meaning in their daily rituals, but I compelled myself to shut up and stay in line, lest people think I was crazy. I pulled out of my depression by repressing it all, by sitting in my silly classroom, by clinging to my role of chronicler.

My father's terrible experience in the work world spurred me to go on to college. I vowed never to subject myself to the indignities he had had to undergo. Nevertheless, the summer after he quit work, when I was seventeen, I accepted a job in the hotel where he had worked. I was hired as a room-service waiter, nonunion, because I was a distant relative of the owner. I was a white among blacks and Puerto Ricans, but they accepted me immediately because they had liked my father. There were men there with ten kids making the same 95 cents an hour that I was. Not only that, but they had to call every man "sir." I didn't, because I was white and didn't plan to make a career out of being a waiter. I also began to realize the basis for black and Puerto Rican anti-Semitism. All of the owners were Jewish, and they fitted the greedy, stingy stereotype so well that they were parodies of themselves. Well before the term "pig" became popularized I referred to them as the "three little pigs." During a banquet at the hotel a guest died of a heart attack. One of the three got up and implored everyone else to "have a good time" in order to make sure that he sold enough liquor.

As a freshman at Brooklyn College I sought to overcome some of my isolation by submerging myself in activities. Since I was more anonymous there, I had more of a chance to become what I wanted to become. I became involved with the antituition committee (political action, 1963 style), tried out for the freshman baseball team, and joined a house plan, sort of a bush-league fraternity. One year I even served as social chairman, in charge of arranging very serious little mixers where, ostensibly, we would meet our partners for life. But I couldn't adjust to the same social system I was mocking. More and more I removed myself from the balls-crushing security hunger of the Jewish middle class, and had little desire to return.

I became interested in politics, as an observer, not an activist. I was a liberal—I felt things were changing gradually, that the political system was slow but effective. During my first year in college I became interested in political science. I liked the collegiate atmosphere in the first course I took. Students spoke analytically, with an "above the fray" condescension, punctuating their points with their pipes. One Friday afternoon, shortly after one of these distant, objective discussions, I heard that President Kennedy had been shot and killed.

That night I felt a severe emptiness, as if my world had come apart. I had viewed Kennedy as any other politician, with a great degree of skepticism. Yet in spite of myself, I had been swept up in the excitement and the idealism he projected. Perhaps I identified with the liberal intellectuals who formed his brain trust. Perhaps I was looking for any positive sign after the vacuous Eisenhower years. The assassination made me realize that America was not immune from unrest. More important, it helped topple me from my perch of "objectivity."

The events following the assassination—the investigation of the crime, the murder of the civil rights workers, the increased involvement in Vietnam—helped crystallize my growing disillusionment with the political system. I came to oppose the Vietnam war not so much because of its cruelty as because of its stupidity. I sadly realized that the Kennedy intellectuals I had admired so much were responsible for this policy.

My radicalization continued, but I stood apart from most radical ideologies. One year, along with members of the Du Bois Club, I went down to Washington to a demonstration. I overheard two of the club members talking about a student whom they called bourgeois. At the time I wore none of the outer trappings of a budding radical—I had short hair, dressed in madras shirts and penny loafers, and wore sunglasses. I felt their pompous narrowness would never win them converts.

Even as my feelings against the war became stronger, I avoided most radical political groups. Yet opposition to the war was for me, and many others, a watershed. As we analyzed the war's causes more thoroughly, we had a more difficult time remaining in America's mainstream. As I prepared to graduate from college, I began to feel part of a nebulous movement—people who were determined to shatter the mythology that had made the war possible.

2. Teaching at McKinley

By the time I graduated, I had decided to leave the provincial sophistication of New York. I planned to teach but had no desire to spend a good part of my life trying to go up the down staircase, aspiring to eventual principalhood. I purposely didn't take the test for a New York teaching license—I didn't even want a choice. When I was accepted by the Antioch-Putney Graduate School, I had no real plans. I was going to try teaching to see what it was like.

Flying to Ohio that summer was a great liberating experience for me. As my day of departure approached, I became more and more afraid of flying. I quickly realized that my fear, like my fear of infinity, was really a fear of living. I was scared to death of being uprooted from New York's ugly womb and thrust onto the Ohio plains. I remembered sitting in Prospect Park as a child and shuddering at the vast sky. Growing up in the city made me feel intimidated by open space. Despite its ugliness, I felt more secure in the city.

I spent the summer of 1967 at Antioch College in Yellow Springs, Ohio, in a raucous, manic dorm. A perceptive undergraduate described the scene as "staying high, talking shit, and getting credit for it." I viewed the summer as a vacation. I called the school Camp Antioch and referred to the professors as Uncle Roy, Uncle Ben, Uncle Phil. I rarely rose before noon and spent afternoons alone reading. Then at night I would smoke up an appetite, eat a chiliburger at the C-shop, or beer and pizza at Com's, and finally cop some doughnuts at the Midnight Bakery. All this hardly prepared me for a year of teaching in an inner-city school. But I wasn't thinking very seriously about the coming school year, probably because the prospect of teaching was so frightening.

Toward the end of August Antioch informed me that I would be working in Washington as an Urban Teacher Corps intern—teaching two sections and attending seminars twice a week. Everyone I spoke to told me how lucky I was to be assigned to McKinley, Washington's elite black high school. The principal, a suave black Amherst graduate, took pride in the high percentage of McKinley graduates who went on to college. Admittedly, he was trying to prove a black school could be "as good as any white school."

This was the fall of 1967, shortly after the federal court decision on segregation in the D.C. school system. In 1967, despite the 1954 Supreme Court decision, the predominantly white schools received the greatest portion of school funds. But only 10 percent of the kids in the D.C. schools were white. Judge Skelly Wright ruled that the "tracking system," which placed kids in academic or nonacademic tracks very early in their school careers, was unconstitutional. Kids were tracked on the basis of race and income. Whites and more well-to-do blacks were placed in academic tracks, while the majority of kids remained in the lower tracks. The tracks were nearly always immutable; a kid remained in his track through high school—if he got that far. The tracking system, reinforced by the inequitable distribution of funds, guaranteed the average black child in D.C. an inferior education.

Former Superintendent of Schools Hansen justified the tracking system in an article in the *Atlantic* (November 1960) this way:

> *Honors Level:* "To protect the quality of instruction, the honors curriculum is selective. A student is enrolled in this curriculum only if he has demonstrated ability to do superior work by his previous grades, testing, and by teacher judgment."
>
> *Regular College Preparatory:* "While this program is designed as preparatory for college, it offers excellent general background for able students not planning college careers. If I could be, or wanted to be, fully authoritarian on this point, I would require every capable pupil, college bound or not, to choose this or the honors curriculum. The intellectual development most needed for general citizenship can best be obtained through study of the great and significant disciplines taught at a demanding and invigorating level. Many students are underachieving, and maximum persuasion, short of authoritarian controls, should be used to motivate them to move up to the more difficult but richer curriculums."
>
> *General Curriculum:* "Viewed as a cafeteria-type selection of subjects with bargain-basement rummaging for good grades at reduced prices."
>
> *Basic Curriculum:* "This curriculum is for the academically delayed high school student, as indicated by standardized test scores in reading and math, academic grades and teacher opinion . . . The two objectives of this curriculum are to upgrade the academic achievement of retarded pupils and provide education for those whose innate endowments, so far as they are reflected in performance, limit the range and difficulty of learning."

A week before classes began, the administration scheduled departmental meetings in every school in the city to figure out how to implement the court decision. The 1967 model rhetoric was full of such terms as "individualized instruction," "curriculum development," "making social studies relevant," and so forth. Those of us too young to know better took these phrases seriously. At the first social studies department meeting of the year the nine Urban Teacher Corps interns and a few other young teachers stood firm for an "open curriculum." Each teacher would determine his own plan for teaching—many of us wanted to use a problems approach instead of the chronological-history curriculum. Some of the social-studies stalwarts were shocked. "You mean," one said with tears in his eyes, "you won't be through the Civil War by January?"

At a faculty meeting earlier in the day the principal suggested that we institute a pass-fail system on an experimental basis. We actually took him at his word. The proposal was too much for the older teachers in the department to take, but we had enough support to push it through. And this was only the first day! But we were naïve about high school politics. Just as we were feeling most triumphant, the assistant principal walked in and began rapping about "thinking it through," "procedure," and the like. The motion was tabled, never to be discussed again.

I was dismayed by how well the kids had assimilated the values of public school, how easily they accepted the blinders that the school had manufactured. One class insisted that we use a textbook and have a quiz every Friday. When I looked over the text I was enraged by its self-righteous half-truths. I decided to use the text in this class, but to approach it critically to help kids develop analytic skills.

In a section on the development of the American colonies the textbook claimed that Georgia was founded out of "man's love for his fellow man," because it gave debtors a chance to leave prison. I prodded students to analyze this statement. "How much of what we do is done out of love for our fellow man? Do Safeway stores run on this basis?"

Gradually kids began to express some of their real feelings. They knew from personal experience that "man's love for his fellow man" often masks motives of self-interest. "Maybe the debtors were removed because it cost too much to keep them in prison," one kid suggested. Another thought that when the debtors became landholders they would be able to repay their debts. I was pleased that they were analyzing the text, an authority they usually took for granted.

But when I used this question on the Friday quiz, at least one person repeated the textbook answer. When we reviewed the test, the girl who had done this protested that the answer was "right here in the textbook."

"Denise," I answered, "you were here for the classroom discussion. The whole class decided to ignore the textbook statement. You could have used common sense."

"Mr. Bhaerman," she protested, "you didn't tell us to use common sense on this test!"

She felt cheated, not because she had given the wrong answer but because two authorities, I and the text, were in conflict. Denise didn't care about the content of the lesson, only about getting a good mark. She was confused, because most of her teachers would have rewarded her for giving the textbook answer. I later saw this pattern repeated by kids who handed in reams of stuff copied from the encyclopedia. Did teachers accept that? Or did they just not bother to read it? Clearly the school rewarded the most obedient, not the most creative students.

Consequently kids never made any connection between what they studied and their own lives. While discussing the Revolutionary War I asked the class whether they would take up arms against a government that taxed them without allowing them representation. Many kids said they would.

"Well, what are you waiting for, then?" I asked. The kids looked puzzled. "Look," I said, "the District of Columbia has no government of its own, no elected representatives in Congress, yet your families pay taxes. If that isn't taxation without representation, I don't know what is!"

Before long I began to see the basic dishonesty of the "innovative" method of teaching. These toys and gimmicks—tape recorders, videotape machines, overhead projectors—all served as sugar to make the medicine go down, a means of making unpalatable subject matter more interesting, hence more digestible. Instead of changing the subject matter to coincide with the needs of the kids, teachers were conning kids into absorbing irrelevant material. Some kids instinctively reacted against this manipulation—they fiercely guarded what little privacy they had. When I asked one student to do a project on anything he was interested in, he answered, "I'm not interested in anything."

What he really meant was, "I'm not interested in anything I could talk to *you* about or anything having to do with schools."

I found little in innovative education that changed teachers' manipulative roles. What was hailed as the "discovery method" of teaching, I realized, was nothing more than a reverse lecture. The teacher guided the discussion by asking the "right" leading questions until the student got the "right" answer by himself, a curiously Skinnerian approach to social studies. While pretending to be nondirective, the teacher in fact perpetuated the deductive method of teaching.

Perhaps the most insidious and harmful aspect of the new social studies is the myth of objectivity and the fetish of scientific investigation. In the hands of most school systems, "rational analysis" serves only to give kids more ammunition to defend their old prejudices, to make them more sophisticated advocates of the American system. The new curricula rarely question the fundamental values of our society.

I had an opportunity to observe this phenomenon firsthand when Joel and I were visiting a "hip, progressive" school in New England that spring. Kids lounged around the spacious campus wearing jeans, beads, and long hair. It looked like Macdougal Street until I got closer. Then I noticed the hippies were remarkably well scrubbed. When I mentioned we were social studies teachers, the office suggested that we visit a very exciting world-history class. We walked in and discovered a lively debate on whether or not Louis XIV had been good for France. The participants were animated and well informed. But I realized that it didn't matter one way or another whether Louis had been good, bad, or ugly. All that mattered was the debate technique. The most effective debater, we are told, is one who can argue successfully for a cause he abhors.

Just as McKinley kids were taught to be bureaucrats and consumers, to be responsive to responsible leadership and television pitchmen, so the upper-middle-class kids were learning
the more sophisticated skills of sophistry, which they could use
to sell an inferior soap or an unpopular war.

Dispassionate analysis also tends to present a false dichotomy between feeling and rationality. How else can terms like
"overkill" "caseload" and "pacification" be made acceptable? I
recall another class, a discussion of the Vietnam war, in which
I asked people if they could kill a member of the NLF. Very
few of the kids felt able to kill a man point-blank, yet nearly
everyone said he would feel comfortable working in a muni-
tions factory. No blood here—just metal and bolts. I tried to
explain that the killer in a technological society was not necessarily just the man who pulled the trigger—but all the people
who had been mobilized to make that act possible.

Proponents of curriculum reform argue that a discussion of
this type actually helps to change consciousness. But no matter
what happens in class, kids will never develop a real sense of
responsibility, a sense of consequences, as long as their schools
are operated by a faceless bureaucracy in which no one really
accepts responsibility for his actions. Instead of giving kids
strength to confront the bureaucracy, innovative teaching
makes them more flabby. Jerome Bruner warns in an article in
Psychology Today that an overly enriched environment might
turn the child into a passive consumer: "A rich and dazzling
environment surely doesn't go very far. The child must do
something on his own about that environment. He has to operate, as it were, on his volition rather than in reaction to what
is happening."

Even the most well-meaning innovative projects are doomed
to fail as long as they are done within the public school framework. I tried to make assignments voluntary, but realized this
was unworkable in a competitive system where all other assignments were mandatory. Five hours a week in my class could
not change kids substantially, especially when their other
teachers reinforced the old values. A kid who had learned to
value the "mark" would do his required work first and have

little time left for other reading. Kids expected me to play the role of a teacher, to entertain them and tell them what to do. When I gave them an assignment to "write about anything you want to," most of the students couldn't do it. Past learning held them with an iron grip.

Classroom discussions were often interesting but mostly irrelevant. The real learning took place in the interaction between the school and the student—the public school medium was the most important message. By the time they got to high school most kids had learned that if they kept quiet and did their work, no matter how silly it appeared, they would be rewarded with a diploma. They were told constantly that McKinley was "their" school, but at the same time the school made it very clear that they had no power to act on any of the conclusions they came to in class or in their student government.

This became clear to me when Ken Hannington, one of the Antioch interns, made the mistake of using an article from *Avant Garde* magazine about four-letter words for a unit on communication. The article itself was innocuous, but it contained the taboo words. Ken made another mistake—he ran it off on the mimeograph machine. The article fell into the hands of an otherwise dormant school board member who was running for re-election. He seized the opportunity to chastise the immoral interns who had no respect for the black community. "If this were a white school he wouldn't do that sort of thing!"

The principal demoted Ken to a nearby junior high school, despite overwhelming support for Ken from the student body. The principal had magnetism—unique for a school administrator. In a system of senile bureaucrats who had little positive contact with students, he always gave kids the impression that he was listening. At the height of the "four-letter word" furor, John Sessions, a white school board member, and Julius Hobson, the man who brought the desegregation suit against the school system, attended an assembly and spoke in support of Ken and another teacher who had used the article.

They asked the kids to vote on whether to keep the teachers

or fire them and handed out ballots. The kids voted 1300–50 to keep the teachers. After the vote was tallied and announced, the auditorium erupted with excitement. In the midst of the tumult the principal strode onto the stage and raised his hand for silence. "I understand how you feel about those teachers," he said. "I'll try to do whatever I can. But right now what I really want to say is . . . we have to go out and Win That Basketball Game!"

A loud cheer went up. Einstein could have learned something about transference of energy.

By the end of this affair I decided to leave the school system. I was convinced that white teachers, especially young radicals, did not belong in the predominantly black system. The D.C. school system resembled a colony, run by the ideal colonial administrators, blacks who had been educated within the segregated system. Protective of their positions, insecure about their authority, they often were more repressive and harsh than their white counterparts had been. Those black teachers who cared about the kids tried to make them tough. In their experience, only the strong survived.

The Urban Teacher Corps sends into this system young, glamorous, well-educated white teachers who are protected by a separate administrative hierarchy, given attractive materials to use, and have only half the teaching load. Yet few interns stay. Older teachers, who had spent a great part of their lives in the school system, thought of us as spoiled and transient, there only to avoid the draft or get a degree.

The interns as a group made few attempts to communicate with the other teachers. The very first day our supervisor, himself a product and perpetrator of this inert school system, helped to isolate us by telling them that we would be Innovating, Developing Curricula. He said it as if we held the secret of the H-bomb and didn't really expect other teachers to understand.

I regarded most of the teachers there as gossipy and petty, the same kinds of people I saw destroying minds in the New York school system. Many black teachers wanted change, but feared losing their positions. I considered them cowards. I continually flaunted my white hippiehood. I refused to wear a tie, let kids call me by my first name, sat cross-legged on the desk. All of this seemed harmless and natural for me, but many kids and teachers saw it as a lack of seriousness, as an affront to the community. By bringing my alienation into the classroom, I hoped to confirm the suspicion that white radical teachers were undermining morality.

I was also disappointed with my own classes. I found it hard to give freedom to kids who had been so strictly controlled in the past. I began to tighten up the classroom discipline, just as many other disillusioned "free" teachers do. Naturally I remained in the teacher role. I still had to evaluate kids, only I reinforced different types of behavior. Instead of rewarding copied garbage from the encyclopedia as other teachers apparently did, I rewarded original work, no matter how garbled or ungrammatical. I wanted to reinforce any attempt at communication, because the school had consciously deprived kids of that skill.

By the end of the year practically all of the kids were writing in their own idiom. I was surprised at the intelligence hidden by the teacher-student barricade. One of the kids wrote a frightening account of a night he spent in jail. Another likened himself to Camus' Stranger, who felt apart from people wherever he went.

I had definitely broken down some barriers. But what if next year's teacher did not accept ungrammatical work? I could afford to discuss alienation and communication—I was white and had an education. For some of these kids, finishing school was a life-or-death project. In a milieu where the choice is work or crime, a high school diploma, no matter how ill-gotten, at least gives people a choice. Nevertheless I respected the hustler, the cynic, even when he hustled me. I found so little healthy spirit in the school that I got a vicarious thrill from rebellious students.

I decided to leave the public school because I didn't want to be a white radical who used the excitement of black revolution to fill a void in his own life. I had become tired of talking to kids about black power when a black should have been doing it. Nor did I want to teach in a school system where I was treated like a baby. When the principal began to complain vaguely about my dress habits, I went to his office to talk. Finally he said, "It's unprofessional not to wear a tie."

"What?" I asked. "Is it professional for me to punch a clock here every day? Or be a hall monitor?"

I realized I didn't want to be an employee, white-collar or any collar. A college diploma did not exempt me from drudgery or chicken shit. I was part of the new working class and wanted no part of it.

Friends who had decided to stay on in the school system argued that it was the only way to change things. "If you leave, then you lose your chance to make a dent. Things go on very smoothly without you." "They go on very smoothly with you too," I suggested. I noticed that teachers who remained in the school system for a few years came to resemble the system rather than the other way around. It takes a remarkable amount of energy to resist the petty oppression you are faced with each day. Many times in my classroom I acted in an authoritarian way. Both kids and administrators were used to this sort of behavior, but I didn't want to play this role. Nor did I want to watch kids be destroyed, knowing how little I could do.

In the spring I became attracted to the school that Joel was working on. I was eager to teach in a more personal, noncoercive way. More important, the school appealed to me because of the physical freedom it promised, freedom from schedules and neckties. When I returned from work at McKinley I was exhausted, not from overwork, just from living my life by an externally imposed clock. Usually I would go to sleep immediately or go out drinking and then go to sleep. Weekends I tried desperately to enjoy myself, becoming more uptight as Sunday wore on.

Just as my students did schoolwork in an alienated way to get a diploma, so I found myself working at McKinley for the means to consume, for the few hours of relaxation at the end of the week. I could no longer tolerate this fragmentation. I saw the new school as a place where my life could become integrated, where I could free myself from the worker-consumer cycle.

CHAPTER II

Joel: From Prep School to Free School

A friend of mine once told me he lived his life as if each portion of it were a chapter from *Pilgrim's Progress*. This is the best simile I can find to describe the pace of my own childhood. I was seeking some imagined perfection. I set standards for myself that I absorbed from my parents and from the professional, upper-middle-class culture in which I lived. I was always trying to prove myself in their eyes—especially in the eyes of my father, a successful college teacher and administrator. I wanted to excel in school, to be productive, to get my work done on time. I put such a premium on getting measurable results that I had no time to get in touch with my own feelings. I would have been the perfect character for a twentieth-century Bunyan novel. The future, the possibility of grace, interested me more than the present.

I had such a compulsion to do well that I could never relax. Slowing down, spontaneity, were obstacles to performance, to attaining the rewards that were the keys to professional success. I renounced my own needs, spent my energies trying to please my faceless taskmasters. But I was also my own best taskmaster. I learned to repress myself. I punished myself when I did poorly and massaged my ego when I did well. I had invested so much of my fragile ego in the rituals of the classroom that I was terrified by the possibility of defeat. Yet the standards I set for myself were so exacting that sometimes it was easier to fail than to conform to them.

I can be lucid about all this now, but at the time schooling mystified me. Education was a given in my life, especially in our academic milieu—a process whose political function I had yet to understand. The terrible psychic price you paid for it, I assumed, was just part of growing up, of becoming an upper-middle-class American.

My parents reinforced the precepts I was learning in school. They were from radically different backgrounds—my father from an immigrant Jewish family, my mother from a Yankee Protestant one—but both had great reverence for academic achievement. They both had done very well in school, and I wanted and was expected to follow their example.

For my father education was the vehicle that had carried him out of the poverty of the Brownsville ghetto in Brooklyn and, ultimately, after several years of work and the Army, to Yale College. He was the only one in his large family to graduate from high school or college—and then only through courtesy of the G.I. Bill of Rights. After a hard day's work his mother would wash and iron his white shirt so that he could go to class impeccably neat. Being clean and well dressed—always above reproach—was his way of overcoming ethnic prejudice. He had to look twice as immaculate as everybody else. He placed such a great importance on neatness that my brother and I rebelled by dressing in a casual, sloppy way. When I was a kid he used to yell at me if my hair was improperly combed, if my shirt was not well ironed.

He was proud of his Jewish heritage, although he was discriminated against because of it. He also impressed on us how hard he had to struggle to overcome the conditions of poverty in which he grew up. I am sure that my later identification with the black struggle sprang partly from my consciousness of my own father's background.

Admission to Yale must have meant a great deal to him. His achievement would help to protect him from the economic hardships and prejudice that were the scourges of his childhood. He always spoke glowingly of Yale, of its intellectual rigor, its spacious surroundings, of the teachers who counseled and taught him. Almost unconsciously I began to imagine that Yale was a kind of "city on the hill," the supreme achievement of American education. I grew up in the shadow of Yale in a lower-middle-class neighborhood in New Haven while my father struggled to support a family and finish his B.A. and doctorate. Most of the older people I met when I was a kid were students or teachers in the university. My mother talks of wheeling me in a baby carriage across the Yale campus. One of my most vivid memories as a child was attending my father's commencement ceremonies with my mother and grandparents.

My mother's parents were freethinking Unitarians from New England who could both trace their genealogy back to America's earliest settlers. My grandmother had relatives who came over on the Mayflower. They imbued my mother with the values of the Protestant ethic, and she applied herself to learning with Yankee zeal. Her failure to win Phi Beta Kappa at Smith was to her a severe blow. She constantly impressed upon my brother, sister, and me the importance of frugality, hard work, and honesty. She warned us against the dangers of self-indulgence. Excessive drinking, smoking, eating were pleasures that would sap energies we should channel into hard work. A model of integrity, she went out of her way never to lie or to cheat. I learned from her how to ration my emotions and that building character was like balancing a bankbook.

Her father, a successful businessman, exemplified all these virtues. Through drive and entrepreneurial skill he founded a wax-novelty company in Buffalo, New York, that made everything from chocolate-filled Easter bunnies and wax mustaches to Nih-I-Nips. He grew up in a farm town in New England where his father had worked at the mill. He knew what it was to be poor and yearned for material success. He wanted to distinguish himself from relatives like his Grandfather Green, a "sloppy, slovenly" man who lacked the drive and self-respect needed to get ahead. He believed that education was one of the keys to upward mobility and ascribed much of his own success to his excellent record in school—he always scored at the top of his class. Having achieved the goals he set out for himself, he assumed that anyone intelligent and industrious enough could do the same.

The son of a Yankee and a Jew, I felt driven to succeed. I always lived in university communities—first in New Haven, later in New Brunswick (when my father worked at Rutgers) —in a milieu that, to use the words of Northrop Frye, seemed "free, classless, and urbane." The academy was the only culture I ever knew. I had no ethnic or religious roots. I had few real ties with either my father's or mother's relatives. We lived in a comfortable house that had a study full of books. Students and teachers visited us constantly. They discussed issues in serious, erudite tones. My father schooled me on *The New York Times,* whose Sunday edition I read dutifully. He used to quiz me on the contents of the "News of the Week in Review." I never questioned the *Times'* reporting, never doubted its claims to fairness and objectivity.

Academics, I assumed, approached the world with disinterested rationality. They soared above the muddy conflicts of the material world. If they had any strong political commitment or class biases, I couldn't discover them. By the time I went to high school I had made the values of my parents and the university elders my own. I especially wanted to please my father, to be the model son—a scholarly young man who would excel as he had.

I spent four years at the Taft School, a New England prep school, the wrong place for a person so guilt-ridden, so anxious to please. The school played on my drive to succeed and reinforced it in a perverse way. It was a chilly, ascetic place that strove to make Christian gentlemen of the sons of America's ruling class. The masters of the school regulated our lives from morning to bed. They organized our days around required study halls, classes, jobs, exercise. We had Vespers services every night and required church on Sunday—the one day that we could miss breakfast and sleep to 8:30 A.M. All of Taft's major functions went on in one large building. During the winter you never had to go outside if you didn't want to. Frightening self-sufficiency! Several times a year the school sponsored carefully chaperoned tea dances with the local finishing schools for women—Ethel Walker's, St. Margaret's—to break up the routine of our all-male culture. One year the administration wanted to ban the twist from the prom but finally relented. We could unleash more energy on the playing fields than the stiff decorum of a tea dance ever allowed.

The regimen of the school was calculated to make us honor and respect our elders, learn manners and social graces, and feel guilty when we broke the rules. Our headmaster, Mr. Cruikshank, was a gentleman in his sixties, who led us with his hand planted on his chest in singing the school song, "O kind, firm moulder of a thousand boys" ("Mother of destinies, dear, lovely place . . ."), at Vespers. He insisted on good manners—an important part of his program of building character in young men. Waiters who served at his table were terrified of making the smallest mistake. Students who sat there had heard stories of the penalties he meted out to those who spilled milk, and acted accordingly.

We learned to be subservient to authority—that was the way to survive at Taft. Like clockwork, we stood up when a master arrived to preside at the dinner table or when he entered the room. Addressing teachers as "sir" became second nature to us. Disobeying their authority brought severe sanctions. They had the power to give out soaks—punishment for infractions of the rules. Too many soaks could lower your "citizenship" grades, put you in study hall, keep you from taking a weekend. Some masters took great joy in catching boys with their lights on after bedtime. One man would take off his shoes and walk in his stocking feet the better to catch his victims.

The more guilty we felt, the easier it was to keep us in line, the more smoothly the school operated. We were constantly reminded of the punishment that would follow our transgressions. Whenever a student got caught for smoking, drinking, cheating, or lying about attending church, the dean or some other school official would make a dramatic example of his case. We learned to know the scoundrels in our midst. Taft had an honor code—the Pledge System—that specifically covered conduct in examinations but in theory applied to all aspects of school life. Every time we finished an exam we had to write, "I pledge my honor as a gentleman that I have neither given nor received aid on this examination." Rumors were always floating around that the Honor Court had summoned some culprit to a basement classroom late at night.

I felt like a true alien during my four years at Taft. I felt awkward among the polished sons of the Wasp elite—kids who had grown up in the bedroom communities of Scarsdale, Winnetka, Darien. Many of them, I imagined, had been going to cocktail parties since the age of twelve. They had wardrobes my parents could never afford. I experienced a combination of hatred and envy when they sported themselves in their best madras jackets.

I stood apart as an absentminded intellectual, the son of an academic in a group preparing for a life of business. I was a perfect target for kids who liked to taunt anyone different from themselves. Some mocked me because they thought I was Jewish, others attacked me for my political views. I didn't have a clear ideology at the time, but I had inherited from my father a faith in the New Deal tradition and a commitment to the underdog. I got my first political education from watching the Army-McCarthy hearings with him. I identified with the men whom the senator from Wisconsin and his cohorts were reviling. My classmates resented my support for blacks, about whom they made snide remarks, and opposed my stand on civil rights and civil liberties. A class-conscious group of future managers, they loved to snub the school's workers, whom they called "bos" and "wombats." They talked derisively of the "townies" from Watertown, the untutored mob who lacked their social graces. In their eyes I was a "New Dealer," a "progressive," who carped at the blessings of the American system.

Yet for all my political awareness, I was a dutiful citizen who played by the rules. My concern for the liberties of others did not extend to my own plight as a student on the academic treadmill. I made the masters of the school my surrogate parents—guides in my quest for perfection. I accepted their authority unquestionably and felt guilty when I didn't come up to their standards.

I was so eager to please, to do what was right, that I created roadblocks for myself. My classmates, however, learned to hustle, to cut corners. The school was no different from the marketplace they were preparing to enter. They paid lip service to "good citizenship" but knew that success had nothing to do with following these high-sounding words. Taft taught them a lesson in practical ethics—that the existence of standards gave legitimacy to a system governed by self-interest.

But I took these standards, the moral strictures, literally, like a son fearful of disobeying the policies laid down by his father. I felt the same mixture of fear and reverence for the masters that I did for my father when he demanded that I do a scrupulous job of mowing the lawn. I carried my fears of disobedience to the point of absurdity in my last year at Taft when I started imagining that I was not following the honor system to the letter. One day I started confessing imagined acts of plagiarism to the Director of Studies—a man who was for me the embodiment of rectitude. I wanted to be reprimanded for my transgressions, but he could only respond with a sense of amazement, almost disbelief. He must have asked himself how anyone could take the rules so literally.

Success scared me. Whenever I came close to attaining it I had to invent some error or sin to explain my accomplishments away. Thus my intense conscientiousness. Trying to do well in the competitive atmosphere of Taft was like trying to scale a cliff and getting a case of vertigo whenever you got too close to the top. The heights were reserved for people like my father, not for me. My bizarre behavior at Taft reminds me of a story a friend told about the guy in the Army who, when ordered to paint a jeep, painted all parts of it—including the tires and headlights.

After completing Taft I went on to Yale, as many of my classmates did. It was the school Taft "prepared" one for. I would be following my father to the university where he had studied. It would be a return to childhood. I had great expectations. I dreamed of an intellectual utopia where people like myself—people of scholarly zeal—would thrive. But I quickly became disaffected when I realized that most of the students did not share my aspirations or ideals. They had come to Yale to prepare for a career. They were there to become members of the governing class. No one had hoodwinked them into coming there. They knew what they wanted and understood that it was Yale's mission to provide them with it. They hoped to get jobs as corporation lawyers, businessmen, bankers, doctors.

Yale accustomed us to a style of life that members of a future elite could rightly expect and even demand. The president addressed us as future leaders, and our plush surroundings gave power to his words. We lived in nice suites in ivy-draped colleges modeled on those of Oxford and Cambridge. The college had spacious grounds, always nicely trimmed and well kept, and all the facilities, that one could ever want. The luxurious paneled dining rooms served bountiful meals. There were always seconds and thirds on everything. We got used to eating long, leisurely meals and to having long conversations over coffee and tea, well into the early evening.

Everything was designed for our comfort and ease. Even the library had a special room called Linonia and Brothers—at that time reserved for men—that had soft reclining chairs and couches for quiet reading and relaxation. We were learning that society reserved boundless space for people like ourselves to use and control. Leisure time would be ours for the asking. We would never feel hemmed in, restricted, harassed by the clock.

These were lessons that our curriculum could never so effectively teach. Our classes reinforced the assumptions with which our daily life had already indoctrinated us. We learned myths, theories of the world that never challenged our status as an elite. The dominant doctrine in the Political Science Department, pluralism, denied that America had a ruling class. The pluralists argued that competing factions, whose interests balanced each other out, governed the society.

Students who arrived on campus from small towns in the South and Midwest or from ethnic enclaves in the cities had to work at becoming "Yalies." They learned to smooth out the rough edges in their speech and to dress in a stylishly self-assured way. The well-modulated tones of eastern speech became the cultural norm, J. Press suits the required fashion. Even when students went slumming they dressed with studied casualness—in jackets and pressed Levi's. There was room among the elite for outsiders provided that they were willing to drop their outlandish ways. Even the secret societies—Skull and Bones, Wolf's Head, Scroll and Key—were willing to admit Jews, Catholics, and blacks who had proved themselves on the playing fields, in the classroom, on the newspaper, in the theater. Stripped of ethnic ties, free of local prejudice, Yale men were ready to assume national leadership.

I was astonished at how quickly everyone began to look and talk alike. Be cool, don't sweat it, hang loose—these were the unwritten rules of conduct. In class we learned to play it safe, to mask our feelings under a façade of rationality. Most students looked down on anyone who temporarily lost control—who got excited, angry, or upset about something he was learning. Students came to lectures to be entertained, to hear anecdotes about the weekend's football game. One of my teachers said he felt the constant pressure to tell jokes, to perform like an after-dinner speaker.

Detachment was the appropriate style for students destined to rule. If you could learn to keep your emotions under wraps you could also handle power. You could govern without quivers of pain or fear, without worrying how your actions affected the lives of others. If you had never listened to your own feelings you were more likely to do what you were told. Many of the major architects of the Vietnam war—the Bundys, the Rostows—graduated from Yale. Yale had prepared them for their roles—roles that they could not carry out successfully without stifling their own best instincts. Since Yale had insulated them from the lives of poor people, how could they identify with the suffering of the Vietnamese? Staughton Lynd, who had a short-lived career as a Yale professor, described the typical Yale graduate as a corporation lawyer who did consulting work for the Peace Corps. Service was something you did in your spare time out of a sense of noblesse oblige.

Despite my alienation, I tried to imitate the polished style of my classmates. I, too, considered myself a member of the elite.

For all my discontent, I was unwilling to give up the luxuries that Yale provided. How could I forsake the future that my credentials guaranteed? Or flee from these sumptuous surroundings? People talked about Mother Yale—an apt metaphor for an institution that enveloped you in its warm folds. I saw no real alternative to the life I was leading. There was no student movement on campus that was mounting a campaign against the interests Yale served. Had there been a counterculture to drop into, I am sure I would have joined it. Unchallenged, the Yale ethic was infectious. It seeped into everyone's consciousness—rebels' and careerists' alike. If you rebelled, you did so on terms that the institution could understand and accept. A rebel could still share the values of his class. He might rage against the university and still consider himself a manager, albeit of a radical cause. He might still look on working people—people who lacked his superior knowledge and finesse —with lofty disdain.

I was never an accomplished Yalie. When I tried to mimic the manners of my peers, my act never really came off. I was too self-conscious, too timid, to carry myself as they did. At parties and dances I saw other students use their social skills to captivate women looking for future corporation lawyers as husbands. I scoffed at their cool style, yet I often wished for their poise. Unable to fit in, I ran to the margins of the university and spent my time with the few friends who were as alienated as I was.

I am sure I would have spent my years at Yale tortured by self-pity if I had not become involved in the civil rights movement. My service in the northern ghettos and work in the southern civil rights struggle showed me that I had options. I discovered that there was an alternative to the privileged life style that Yale students were cultivating. I did not join the movement for ideological reasons—because it had the right theory on society. It excited me because it engaged dimensions of my personality that had lain dormant at college. I was bored and restless, tired of playing academic games, of trying to perform to please my parents.

The people in the movement were first and foremost activists who took risks in behalf of their ideals. Their example took me outside the walls that protected us from the ugly conditions of the ghettos nearby. Enjoyment of the comfort and privileges Yale bestowed on us, I realized, required our acquiescence in racism. And dealing seriously with racism demanded that we first acknowledge our responsibility for perpetuating it. It meant giving up our secure status to join the insurgency the prisoners of the ghetto and rural segregation were creating.

One day when walking by Dwight Hall, the Yale YMCA, I noticed a sign that announced a campaign to wear black armbands for James Meredith, who had just been barred from the University of Mississippi. I went upstairs to find out about it and met Peter Countryman, a Yale student who had left school to found the Northern Student Movement. NSM started out as a white college support group for the southern freedom movement, sending food, clothing, and other supplies. It developed into an organization that ran community organizing projects and service programs in the northern ghettos. It was in the forefront of the school boycotts, rent strikes, and mass demonstrations that broke out in the mid-sixties. I wore a black armband and became a close friend of Peter's. He was the only person I knew who led a life that was not defined by the contours of the university. Whenever we got together I sensed the utter unreality of my own life. Once when we were eating together in the Calhoun College cafeteria, Peter commented on how few people enjoyed the bountiful meals we did. I winced when he said this, realizing how much I took Yale's largesse for granted. Peter later went back to Yale to study political science, but only to pick up the skills and knowledge to make him a better organizer.

As a result of conversations with Peter I began to think seriously about the conditions blacks lived under and what I could do to change them. I joined a discussion group that Peter and Joan, his wife, organized to deal with the dynamics of racism. I also began working in the tutorial programs that Dwight Hall ran in the community schools of New Haven. Now I was using my knowledge in a concrete way to serve kids beaten down or neglected by the New Haven school system.

Tutoring was pretty tame compared with my experience working for the civil rights movement in St. Augustine, Florida, during the summer of 1964. It was "freedom summer" in the South, the time when countless white college students left their campuses and suburban homes to work for SNCC, SCLC, and CORE.

St. Augustine, the oldest city in America, was a most unlikely battleground. A tourist capital, it attracted northerners who wanted to bathe in the sun and see the sights of the "ancient city"—the oldest jail, the oldest fort, the slave market. The climate was tropical and balmy, the atmosphere placid, the streets lined with cyprus trees. Since it had no industry, St. Augustine's prosperity hinged on its ability to draw these tourists. Any strife, any bad publicity, would hurt the town's "fathers"—the moderate men who owned the banks, the motels, the stores.

Martin Luther King and the SCLC chose St. Augustine as the focal point of their summer direct-action campaign because it was so vulnerable to bad publicity. King wanted to expose the contradictions that the elegant motor courts and hotels hid from the public's eye. For St. Augustine was a segregated city. And it was located in the heart of northern Florida, a stronghold of the Klan, no different from Georgia, Mississippi, or Alabama.

When the local black movement, led by Dr. Robert Hayling, a dentist, tried to attack the town's racist practices through picketing, demonstrations, and sit-ins, violence erupted. Crosses were burned, homes fire-bombed, shotguns fired in the middle of the night. Rural toughs drove through black neighborhoods in the familiar red pickup trucks. When the SCLC came to town, the local version of the Klan—the Ancient City Hunting Club—mobilized to defeat them. The Hunting Club's leader, Hoss Manucy, a huge potbellied man, wore a ten-gallon hat and six-guns. He lived with his large family in a house outside St. Augustine. Pigs wallowed in his yard, which was cluttered with old cars. Manucy's boys traveled in cars that flew Confederate flags and were equipped with two-way radios.

When the first big street demonstrations occurred, Sheriff L. O. Davis deputized the Hunting Club members. Other "outside agitators," notably Connie Lynch, a racist and anti-Semite from California, and J. B. Stoner, vice-president of the National States Rights Party, arrived to heat up the crowds of white citizens who met nightly in the slave market, the square in the middle of town.

The conflict between the black community and the Klan had all the elements of a melodrama, of a morality play. The demonstrations pitted King's nonviolent army against the unregenerate forces behind Manucy and L. O. Davis. King and his lieutenants never gave up on their opponents, kept trying to convert them to the cause. Nonviolence was a method of making them aware of their sin. As King put it in one of his sermons, "Loving Your Enemies," "Every word and deed must contribute to an understanding with the enemy and release those vast reservoirs of good will which have been blocked by impenetrable walls of hate." When L. O. Davis came to a mass meeting late in the summer, the whole crowd sang out "We Love L. O. Davis." Movement leaders instructed us to shame our opponents by refusing to strike back if they beat us.

The battles that summer transformed famous monuments of the city into arenas of violence. Demonstrators clashed with rednecks and police in the old slave market. When blacks tried to integrate the swimming pool of Monson's Motor Lodge, the owner, James Brock, retaliated by throwing acid into the water. When the movement organized swim-ins, Manucy's raiders clubbed blacks on the silver sands of St. Augustine beach.

I began to understand the forces that were ripping the city apart when Jono Brown, a classmate, and I traveled to St. Augustine in May of our sophomore year. We went there to talk to Dr. Hayling and other black leaders about an educational project we were organizing. We wanted to recruit fifteen to twenty northern college students to teach classes in the black community during the summer. Students from Yale and other New England colleges had gone to jail in St. Augustine during Easter when they joined Mrs. Malcolm Peabody, Rev. William

Sloane Coffin, and other college chaplains in protesting segregation. Since their actions had boosted the morale of the black community, Dr. Hayling had asked people from the colleges to continue their support. The freedom school that Jono and I were planning was a concrete expression of our solidarity with the freedom movement.

I remember vividly our first night in Florida. Jono and I met Dr. Hayling at the airport and began speeding down the highway from Jacksonville to St. Augustine. The doctor began telling us stories of the harassment and brutality he and many other blacks had suffered. Segregationists had fired at his house in the middle of the night. His dental practice, which had once included many whites, was now beginning to suffer. He was growing more and more bitter about the failure of the federal government to investigate or in any way redress the grievances of the black community.

As we drove along the highway Hayling pointed to the spot where the Klan had caught him and three other black men eavesdropping at one of their meetings. They had beaten them with clubs and chains. One Klansman played Russian roulette on the doctor's head. When the police investigated the incident they charged Hayling with assault.

We heard many more stories of violence and met more victims of the terror. One day Jono, the doctor, and I visited the first black man who tried to enroll his children in an all-white school. His penalty: his home burned to the ground. Despite the tremendous repression, we discovered that the black community was far from united in combating their subservient condition. The black educators—the public school teachers and officials of Florida Memorial College—feared the arrival of the SCLC. And they were the people whose support was essential for our project. Their livelihood depended on pleasing the white power structure, their reputation on their role as moderates. They served as buffers between angry blacks and the white community. They would rather sit down to tea with their antagonists or participate on a biracial committee than march in the streets.

When we went to talk with Royal Puryear, the president of

Florida Memorial College, about using the college facilities for the program, he expressed great anxiety about our association with SCLC. He feared that our project would teach propaganda and instruct the young in the art of picketing and in other forms of direct action. His college received a great deal of money from local businessmen and the leading bank of St. Augustine held its mortgage.

Jono and I traveled to St. Augustine again in early summer to lay the groundwork for the tutorial program. We quickly discovered, however, that people's minds were not on education but on the daily picketing and night marches SCLC was leading. If we wanted to gain the trust of the community we could not stay aloof from these struggles. What we had envisioned as a safe venture soon turned into one filled with peril. The day we arrived Hosea Williams told us a chilling story of the night marches at the slave market. White men with ax handles and tire chains had beaten up demonstrators—young and old, men and women—while policemen looked on. When we went to sleep that night we realized we had walked into a tinderbox.

The next night we went to a huge mass meeting at St. Paul's church. It was a turning point for both of us. We had come as spectators, but the singing, chanting, and clapping were contagious. Such songs as "O Freedom" and "I'm Going to Sit at the Welcome Table" drew us into the community. Once the crowd had reached a fever pitch, the SCLC leaders began to speak, exhorting everyone to take action. Hosea Williams asked us, "Are you ready to march tonight?" Neither Jono nor I had come to the meeting expecting to make any such decision. It was not the kind of question that we could answer "objectively." Life in the classroom had not prepared us to make decisions that would have real, personal consequences, that might even put our lives in jeopardy. We felt trapped, bewildered by the insane situation in which we found ourselves. Mostly we felt very scared. But we stepped into line.

It was eight o'clock, the night pitch black, as we headed toward the slave market. Almost immediately bands of brawny youths charged into the line, smashing newsmen's cameras, beating up demonstrators. No sign of police. I eluded the attackers, but some of them pummeled Jono. Our assailants won that night's contest. We never accomplished our goal—to round the slave market and return to the black community.

The next night was even more eerie. This time the four to five hundred of us reached the slave market. Bands of angry whites filled the square. They taunted the few whites in the crowd, called us "white niggers." Their eyes blazed with hate. We had committed the ultimate sin—we had been disloyal to our race.

I encountered the same fury later in the summer when I accompanied a group of blacks to a local restaurant the day Johnson signed the Civil Rights Bill. A man in his mid-thirties came over to our table to jeer at us. He was horrified that I had come to accompany my black friends—he just stared and stared at me. He cursed me, shrieked that I was worse than scum.

The glowering faces of the men in the slave market frightened me. Ugliness and hate were in the air and I expected violence to erupt at any moment. I tried to present a calm appearance, but I felt paralyzed inside. The young blacks in line walked serenely in the face of massive hostility. These kids —sometimes five to ten years younger than me—had a tough, resilient style, the necessary equipment for survival in a southern town. They did not fight back when they were struck or retaliate when missiles were thrown at them. Invariably they rushed to help a comrade who was being beaten up, cushioning the blows by throwing themselves over his body.

Halfway around the slave market, I heard the sound of rocks being crushed and broken into pieces. Bricks and bottles soon began to fly all around us. In panic I dodged out of the way and found myself in a more precarious position. I had lost my place in line and was now standing between a line of police and snarling dogs and the crowd of hostile onlookers. I had no idea of what to do. I felt totally immobilized. As I stood there one of the whites in the crowd jumped me and threw me to the pavement. My glasses flew off. He began kicking me and tearing at my shirt. I pulled myself together and found myself face to face with a cop carrying a club and holding a menacing German shepherd on a leash. The dog kept lunging forward in a vicious way. I felt sure he would bite me. I mumbled something to the cop about being part of the demonstration, and before he could do anything to me, I raced off to rejoin the march. That night my white skin, my elite background, had been no protection against suffering. Yale had numbed my feelings. Now the movement was helping me to let my guard down, to develop the capacity to take risks.

For most of the rest of the summer I worked in a freedom school in two local churches, where I taught English and black history. Twelve of us—mostly students from New England colleges—taught close to a hundred students in the churches and at Florida Memorial College (Royal Puryear had relented and allowed us to use his school's facilities). I rarely stepped out of the black community that summer. It was a refuge from the terror I was sure to experience if I walked downtown. It was exhilarating to feel supported and protected by one's neighbors, people to whom you said hello every day and who smiled back. It was great to be away from the competitive frenzy of the academy. The black neighborhood of St. Augustine was probably the first real community I had ever lived in. Wherever we went—whether to a mass meeting or to the Blue Goose (a local bar)—people who didn't know us made us feel at home. Women generously served us meals at the Elks Rest. Families sheltered us. I felt that I belonged where I was, that I had roots, if only for a summer.

It was an electric experience to walk through the streets at the height of the direct-action campaign. The movement strengthened the bonds between people, sparked a real élan among the youth, who strode through the streets singing and chanting, unafraid. The mass meetings we attended that summer were like revival meetings. They crackled with excitement, with the spirit of camaraderie that only the experience of shared risks can kindle. The songs we sang that summer—

"Which Side Are You On, Boys?," "Going to March on St. Augustine Tonight, My Lord," "O Freedom," "If You Miss Me from the Back of the Bus"—symbolized the communal energy we all felt.

Even though I lived in the black community, I never really felt safe. The day that the volunteers arrived we learned that the Klan planned to march through Washington Street, the main drag in the black community. We huddled together in the Elks Rest, learned the arts of nonviolent self-defense, and peered through the windows, as if waiting for the apocalypse to come. The Klan never marched. Police cars drove past our house at all times of the day and night. We lived in fear of being shot at or of being bombed. I frequently woke up in the middle of the night, mistaking the rustle of trees or some early-morning noise for prowlers.

One night in early summer Jono and I and C. T. Vivian, an SCLC leader, thought we heard the ticking of a time bomb. We went outside to investigate and found that it was only a clock resting on our next door neighbor's windowsill. He got so alarmed when he heard us that he pointed a gun barrel in Jono's face. C.T. assured him that we were brothers, not rednecks out to do him in.

We shared a world with our students. When we weren't working together in class our lives intersected in the streets, in mass meetings, in the courtroom. Freedom school became part of the total fabric of our relationship, not an imposition on them. The things kids wrote about developed organically from the political drama we were all involved in—the mass meetings, marches, sit-ins, swim-ins, the signing of the Civil Rights Bill. Students were learning to express their feelings without fear of reproach, to develop a personal writing style. We talked about Baldwin's *Go Tell It on the Mountain*, about leaving the South to find the promised land in a northern city. Was the ghetto in all its ugliness the way out, was it any better than a segregated southern town, we asked ourselves? This was a real question for these kids, who were captivated by the myth of northern progress, who had friends and relatives in the city.

Most young people left St. Augustine because there were so few opportunities, because life was so dull and flat in the tourist town.

Feeling comfortable about using the first person, about speaking whatever came to mind, were small things to us. But they were major breakthroughs for our students, who had been conditioned to view themselves as dependent human beings. The summer taught me how thoroughly politicized the public schools are. Segregated education, I discovered, was an education for servility. Rote learning, the authoritarian classroom, could best prepare these future "hewers of wood and carriers of water" for their place in southern society.

Going back to Yale was the farthest thing from my mind when the summer was over. Having tasted freedom, having developed a strong commitment to the movement, I had no desire to return to the old cycle of academic labor. I wanted to continue my social activism. I thought of dropping out of school for a year to work for the Philadelphia Tutorial Project, a program of the Northern Student Movement. But my enthusiasm soon waned. My parents, particularly my father, persuaded me to go back to school. Why stop when I only had two years left, he said. So I returned to Yale for my junior year. Looking back on it now, I realized that the experiences of my trip south had been somewhat vicarious. Despite the deep changes I had gone through, I was still fighting for the rights of others. I was more sensitive to the oppression of blacks than I was to the more subtle tyrannies of my own life—school and family.

By my senior year I had grown terribly frustrated with what I was studying at college. I found my studies boring and abstract compared to work in the community or participation in the movement. I enjoyed intellectual work but wanted to find a way to connect it with my political interests. I saw only two alternatives—to become either a scholar-teacher or a full-time activist.

Staughton Lynd, the first teacher I had who really moved me as a person, helped me to work through those conflicts. Unlike many teachers, he did not try to hide his feelings and commitments behind his public role. His interests in scholarship had their roots in his experiences in the South as a teacher in a black college and as SNCC coordinator of the freedom schools in Mississippi. He balanced his time between teaching, writing, and work for the civil rights and antiwar movement. While many teachers spent their days cloistered in the library doing specialized research or jousting at faculty meetings, Staughton found the time to speak at antiwar rallies, to demonstrate, and even to fly to Hanoi. I realized how hostile Yale was to activist teachers who overstepped the bounds of "academic freedom" and "objectivity" when President Kingman Brewster condemned him for speeches he made in North Vietnam. Staughton expressed spirit and joy in an otherwise stuffy place.

Jono and I decided in our senior year to organize our own course with Staughton on "the radical tradition in America." We wanted to study the development of radical movements and ideology in our history. We wrote up a proposal, got it past the guardians of Yale curriculum, and started meeting at Staughton's place for evening seminars. Other Yale activists joined our group. It was exciting to be studying with people who saw intellectual work as a way of becoming more effective agents of social change. Being a radical at Yale was a lonely vocation. Our class provided me with the reinforcement I could get no place else. Doing research on Tom Paine and Gene Debs helped me to understand the genealogy of our movement's programs and values. I discovered men and organizations in our history with whom I could identify, to whom I could look back for inspiration in today's struggles. While we studied the past, we also wrestled with Fanon, Mills, Marcuse, William Appleman Williams, in order to construct an ideology for the present.

I needed more than a study group to survive during my senior year. I wanted to move off campus. Living in a college isolated from the black community was not a good context for the study I wanted to do. The best I could do was to theorize about the strategy and tactics of social change from my room in Calhoun College. I was also growing impatient with the meager results of the work I was doing for Dwight Hall. The tutoring program only grazed the surface of the problems that ravaged the ghetto. I felt that tutoring and other social service programs that Yale students participated in were a form of "welfare colonialism." They made the residents of the community overly dependent on the volunteer. They stifled black people's sense of self-reliance, their capacity to take power in their own behalf. Tutoring, recreation, and other "big brother" programs made things a little more palatable but did not change the structure of power in the black community. And powerlessness was at the root of the oppression that afflicted black Americans. They had no control over any of the institutions that functioned in their neighborhoods—the police, the schools, the urban renewal agency. The white radical student, I reasoned, should be a community organizer, a person who catalyzed struggles for self-determination. This was the strategy that the Northern Student Movement had taken and that the SDS ERAP (Economic Research and Action Projects) were now adopting.

A group of us—eight students—banded together to petition the university to let us live off campus. In order to protect the sanctity of the colleges, university policy allowed only students with psychiatric permission to take apartments. We tried to make our statement a general critique of Yale's education and living arrangements, not simply an appeal on behalf of our special interests: "A community, we submit, does not function by closing itself off from life around it, by making itself an island of placidity in a sea of movement . . . We think, then, that concrete contact with the more mundane side of New Haven life, as differentiated from the academic abstractions which are our fare, would help life at Yale."

In his personal statement John Wilhelm, now a trade union representative in New Haven, explained the philosophy of education that compelled him to leave the campus. Most of us shared his views.

I can't accept the theory that I should build in Yale's secluded imperturbability the intellectual foundations with which I then try to attack the problems of my society . . . It is not possible to grasp intellectually the significance of life in poor, particularly Negro, neighborhoods without partially sharing in that life; it is certainly not possible as a historian—my field is history—to understand the dynamics of social movements generally without understanding the situation from which movements arise and even, I suspect, without participating in movements. It makes no sense to deal with the obvious dichotomy between abstraction as we get it here at Yale and reality as I find it in the Hill by learning the abstractions and then re-evaluating them through subsequent experience.

Most of the members of the committee in charge of evaluating our proposal treated us like "poor little lambs who had lost our way." Weren't we satisfied with life in the colleges, didn't we enjoy their rich social and intellectual activities? In their eyes we were errant students who wanted to leave the fold. The burden was on us to explain why we wanted to leave campus, not on the institution, which had failed to meet our needs. At one point in the meeting Dean May recommended that we should take a medical exam before voyaging into the community. It was as if he felt we couldn't survive the rigors of living outside the residential colleges. May was speaking for Mother Yale, who feared for the security of her children.

Our applications were approved, and two friends and I moved into an apartment in the Legion Avenue area, once an old Jewish neighborhood, now predominantly black. The city had slated many houses in our area for destruction to make way for a highway that would cut a swathe through the neighborhood. Many of the people had been forced to move before, and now the urban renewal agency was ignoring their interests again. Planners were making decisions according to "technical" criteria without consulting the people whose lives would be most drastically shaped by them. We hoped to do community organizing, but in the remaining six months of our school year we had barely enough time to grasp the many problems that swamped our neighborhood. I enjoyed my independence from college; I had never realized how much Yale had dominated my consciousness. Now I was living among people for whom Yale was but a distant reality. I vowed to leave the academy after graduation, but I was not sure what to do.

My roommate, Shel Stromquist, got me interested in going to Africa. He suggested that we go to Dar es Salaam, Tanzania, to learn about the activities of the liberation movement in Southern Africa. All the exiled parties from the white settler countries—Rhodesia, South Africa, Southwest Africa, Angola, Mozambique—had offices in Dar. Thousands of refugees from these countries had come to Tanzania. Few people in the American movement knew about the struggles for nationhood in the southern tip of the continent. By gathering information about those political parties, by making contact with their members, we would be broadening the perspective of American radicals. After returning from Tanzania we planned to write articles, give speeches, and find ways to share our knowledge with groups across the country. Shel really excited me about the idea, but we could find no organization to sponsor our trip. The most likely organization, the American Friends Service Committee, was very interested but thought our proposal was too political.

I decided to go to Tanzania anyway to work with Southern African refugees. I got a job at a secondary school for refugees funded by AID, which was located in a small suburb outside Dar es Salaam. There were students at the school from all the Southern African countries as well as from Tanzania, Zanzibar, and Malawi. They were of all ages—from twelve to thirty-five. The average student, in his late teens or early twenties, had fled his country for political reasons (to avoid arrest), to get an education, or to seek out opportunities blocked to him as a black man in a colonial society. Many had come at great risk, had gone through great ordeals in their journeys. One man told me about trying to escape through the border fences watched vigilantly by South African guards. Another fellow described a seven-hundred-mile journey in which he foraged in the forest and walked great distances with little food and water.

I felt very squeamish about working for the American government. But I wanted to work with refugees and learn about

Southern Africa, and this seemed the only way to do it. I tried to convince myself that I could function independently in spite of the school's government affiliations. I thought I could use AID, but in fact they used me and the other volunteers very effectively. I could teach what I wanted, but I was still working as part of the public-relations campaign America was selling to the Third World.

The school was a showcase, an attempt to show Southern Africans that Americans really cared, that humanitarianism was central to our government's purpose. The government cast us, idealistic men and women, as America's best ambassadors. Never mind that America had large investments in South Africa, or that we gave arms to Portugal, which she used to suppress revolts in Angola and Mozambique. If Southern Africa became independent, AID probably hoped the leaders of these countries would remember America's philanthropic acts and open their doors to corporate capital. We might be mere teachers, but by perpetuating the myth of American benevolence we were helping to fulfill our government's imperial dreams.

The leaders of the liberation groups understood the function of the school very well, saw it as a place where students could hustle skills that would make them more valuable members of the parties. A good number of the students never really trusted us. Whether I remained silent about Vietnam or openly opposed the war, I was still damned in the eyes of most militant students. Nothing I could say sounded authentic to them. They were always looking for my hidden motives. When I was analyzing the UN intervention in the Congo, I blamed the UN for failing to protect Lumumba from his enemies. The UN, I concluded, was in large part responsible for the Congolese leader's death. But a fiery Rhodesian in the class insisted that the UN had plotted to kill Lumumba and that I was deliberately hiding the fact from the class.

Not only my employer but my own cultural and class biases made it difficult for me to serve my students. My affluent, upper-middle-class background, my leisurely education, blinded me to the needs of poor students who were preparing for a life of revolutionary warfare and nation-building. I could afford to be objective, to analyze the world, as if above the fray. But they were participating in a revolutionary movement, in a rapidly accelerating continent, and demanded the tools and knowledge that they could quickly translate into action. They wanted answers, accurate descriptions of social reality, and all I could give them was cautious estimates and cool responses. They were impatient with my attempts to democratize the classroom, to solicit their advice on what we should study. They wanted me to *teach*—to convey my wisdom comfortably, as their party leaders and tribal chieftains did.

They forced me to recognize my failure to take a stand, to openly reveal my biases, when I was teaching. One student told me, "You Americans never say how you really feel." I still wanted to look at both sides of every question, as if the outcome of the investigation didn't really matter. I was afraid to use the word "imperialism" in discussing international politics because it was too emotionally charged for me. The angle of vision from which my students perceived the word was radically different. They saw events as different as the UN intervention in the Congo, the Suez crisis, and the Korean war from their perspective as victims of colonialism, of great power domination. I was still the citizen of a country that controlled 60 percent of the world's resources and I viewed the world from that comfortable position.

I never really understood the crushing impact of colonialism on the lives of my students until I traveled through South Africa and Rhodesia after a year of teaching. A Canadian friend and I hitchhiked through these lands, whose breathtaking beauty—Victoria Falls, the South African coast, Cape Town— contrasted with their savage political systems and the terror of the police state. Our experiences reminded us over and over again that we were white and that skin color was a ticket to either a position in the master race or a life of degradation. Black men and women called us "boss," we traveled on buses that excluded blacks, Indians, and coloreds. All around us in South Africa signs blared in Afrikaans—*Slegs Vir Blankes* (Whites Only).

The whites who picked us up on the highway must have

been afraid to pass us by. I am sure they felt bound to relieve us from our unseemly condition. When we told them that we were American and Canadian tourists, they treated us with courtesy and warmth. One Afrikaner fed us and put us up at his home for the night. But we were living a lie on our journey. We were afraid to tell people our real place of origin, our true vocation, for fear they would turn us in. Sometimes our drivers scared us. We got a lift from a merchant marine man who carried the two of us squeezed into his Alfa Romeo five hundred miles to Cape Town. He was carrying a gun in his glove case to protect him from "Kaffirs."

A visit to a South African gold mine confirmed our students' stories of the exploitation of black labor. Cheap labor was the key to the wealth and prosperity of a regime where most white men could afford to have at least one servant. Our guide, an Englishman dressed in a fashionable blue blazer, talked about how well his company treated the labor force. To hear him, one would think that the company was a model of philanthropy. We cringed when he showed us the huge vats of beer and other yeasty food that they served the workers. High calories make energetic miners. He showed us the squalid compounds where the workers lived and the recreation grounds where they let off steam in tribal dances. By the end of my journey I had grown bitter at the United States government for permitting corporations and banks to invest capital that fueled the power of this racist country. But how could American business pass up the chance to invest under such favorable conditions—cheap labor, a stable social system, a police state to ward off any insurgency?

We saw few signs of unrest in South Africa. Any serious political resistance was taking place underground now that the government had banned all the revolutionary parties. The white liberals we met felt impotent in the face of the heavily militarized state. How could you dare to budge a government that was prepared to crush you at the first hint of dissidence? We saw no policemen and soldiers in the street, for the citizens had silenced themselves.

Three days before the end of our stay two representatives

from the Special Branch, the South African secret police, came to visit my friend and me. We both were amazed at how easily we had crossed the Rhodesian–South African border. Now Intelligence was compensating for the laxity of the customs officials. Both highly polished Afrikaners, they treated us with kid gloves, with diplomatic finesse. They asked us a number of routine questions and discovered that we planned to leave the country in a few days. But they had not come to interrogate us, only to let us know that we were being watched, that the police state was omnipresent. I flew from Johannesburg to New York, happy to have left the poisonous atmosphere of South Africa behind.

I was returning to the States to join the Antioch-Putney Graduate School, whose brochure attracted me with its promise of a year of inner-city teaching. I thought that teaching in a ghetto high school would be an excellent way to continue the work I had done in the civil rights movement and in Africa. Like many other activists my age, I felt that the black community was where the action was. So when Antioch placed me in a predominantly white middle-class high school, Montgomery Blair, in Silver Spring, Maryland (on the outer edge of Washington, D.C.), I was really upset. I imagined that the kids would be soft and complacent, that they would experience none of the anguish that is the common condition of black Americans and Third World people.

I wrote a plaintive letter my first month to the students at Kurasini.

The teaching has been most difficult, as the students do not share the enthusiasm for learning that many of you at Kurasini did. They are well off—their parents have good jobs, nice homes, many students have cars. They do not really feel that they have important problems except perhaps the date with the girl they are going to have on the weekend, or what the football team is going to do on Saturday. Unlike the Kurasini students, they are not very much interested in politics or in international problems. The world outside their comfortable communities does not seem to really affect them. I am teaching two American History courses, and the real challenge is to make the students aware of the painful problems our society is facing—the ugly war outside our borders, the oppression of Negroes in the ghettos of our cities, the military draft that may call them when they reach the age of 18. Yet communicating these problems to them is not easy, as many cannot see, for example, what the cruel treatment our society metes out to Negroes has to do with them.

But my conceptions of the students soon began to change. I discovered that the bland, all-American atmosphere of the school concealed a great deal of suffering. Many kids were virtually suffocating from their routinized existence at Blair. Reciting Shakespeare or learning English vocabulary made little sense to them when they were experiencing acute personal tensions. A drug experience, a romance, a conflict with parents, an interest in the Poor People's Campaign—none of these concerns was a legitimate part of the curriculum. And they had little time to talk to their classmates about the things that were tearing up their guts. They had to focus their attention on the teacher if they were to be ready for the next question.

Jeremiah, one of the radical students at Blair, tried to describe the alienation he saw all around him.

This is a school attended by restless students: students with nothing to look for, except maybe another day of school or a far distant "success."

For many others, high school is a distraction which takes up most of their time, if not with work, then with worry in apprehension of the next day. Many students have not even had the time to think whether they want to participate in this world full of killing, hatred, greed, and poverty. Many question their own existence, their ethics, morals and their destiny, yet they must push these things behind them in their "quest" for knowledge. This is ridiculous. Can you imagine a person who does not know whether he wants to withdraw from society or not do his trigonometry? Where is the relationship of learning to the students? The courses at this school are totally unrelated to these people who are growing in number. Students feel alienated. Some give up, others push blindly forward, groping their way, obtaining "pleasures" from the deviants which the "system" has ingeniously devised to take their minds off their hopelessness; such as parties, sex, drinking, going to the teen club, shooting the bull in a coffee house, messing around in Silver Spring or Georgetown, or generally doing nothing that relates to anything, that is ever discussed in school. Where can the student discuss his Saturday night experiences or his contact with life outside of school within the system of public schools? To what do you relate your learning without any moral or ethical principles, from these experiences? In which class can he discuss with others why he feels lost, in an effort to find himself and become "aware"? An awareness which is so pertinent to his making a better world to live in. An awareness which makes one more than a "good" scientist, teacher, psychiatrist, or economist, or bricklayer, but a "good" man.

There was no space in the school that students could call their own. I would often meet kids who skipped their classes to walk out to the grove, the library, or wander the corridors just to seek out some social contact. The administration tried to rob kids of their rare moments of intimacy. Norman Solomon, a writer for the school paper, describes one such incident during lunch hour in the Blair quadrangle.

> Surrounded by the bricks and school windows, among those resting between rounds of repressions, a pair is locked in tight embrace; sprawled in the quadrangle, oblivious somehow to all the secondary maneuvering and game-playing; shocking—is there something REAL going on HERE, amongst the preparatory trivia?
> The girl is crying.
> > . . . and not about grades or college recommendations.
> > Amazing.
> > Life growing between cracks in the concrete?
> Ah, the automatically anticipated, seemingly inevitable . . .
> "All right, Charlie, not here. This isn't Rock Creek Park."
> Whispered: "What did he say?" Almost insane enough to be incredulous.
> "All right, Charlie. Not here."
> And a cry and scream mixed together: "Please leave us alone!"

That fall a number of students asked me to serve as a sponsor for an organization they wanted to start, the Student Organizing Committee. They wanted to set up a discussion group that would deal with issues that were banished from the curriculum—the draft, race, rock music, experimental education. But the administration felt threatened by a group that would be organizing independently of the official channels. The school already had a Cultural Activities Committee run by the Student Government which sponsored lectures and debates, and the principal argued that SOC would be usurping its functions. The Cultural Activities Committee, we discovered, was a dead-letter group. It rarely organized any activities in the school.

The principal could not have liked the role he assumed I would play in the organization. The faculty adviser was supposed to mediate between students and the administration, not advocate their interests. I was not willing to be a moderating force in SOC, to be there to introduce a note of caution whenever the kids got too self-reliant. Many of the faculty did not like the close, personal ties that were developing between me and the kids. A faculty member, they felt, should maintain his distance. Later in the year the principal told me that some teachers had complained to him about my "unprofessional conduct." They had seen me sitting on the floor talking with some students.

Our first clash with the administration developed when one of the organizers of SOC placed copies of Jerry Farber's article "Student as Nigger" on some of the school's bulletin boards. An attached sheet announced that SOC (still not an official school organization) would sponsor a discussion of the article after the end of classes. I discovered, much to my surprise, that I had been slated to lead the discussion. The fellow who put it up had forgotten to tell me his plans. When the administration found out, they panicked. The article, they claimed, would inflame racial tensions at the school. And all posters required their approval before being tacked onto school bulletin boards. The assistant principal told us to take down the posters and cancel the meeting. We caved in to his demands.

For much of September and October several of the SOC organizers and I had an endless round of discussions with the principal about the formation of SOC. He wanted to know whether we intended the group to be a discussion rather than an action organization. The name disturbed him, and he wanted us to find a milder-sounding title. We told him that it was impossible to separate critical thought and discussion from action. Talk that had no practical consequences for one's own life was not what we wanted. We refused to change its name.

The principal told us he feared we would only present one side of an issue. The school's function, he said, was to make a balanced presentation of all social problems. He implied that Montgomery Blair was an institution above politics and that SOC was a partisan organization bent on injecting militance into the school's tranquil halls.

I learned that year how the rhetoric of "objectivity" could mask real bias and self-interest. The Montgomery County School system had very clear political objectives. It tried to limit dissent by prohibiting the circulation of leaflets and the posting of announcements without prior permission. It rarely gave permisson to anyone who wanted to distribute controversial material—on the draft, the war, student rights. Schools cooperated with the Selective Service System by sending the names of graduating seniors to their draft boards. If you tried to present a radical perspective in the classroom, other teachers might accuse you of indoctrinating your students. In a lecture on the labor movement in American civilization I compared the public school to a factory. The leader of our teaching team, a woman of liberal politics, argued that this was a "biased" interpretation.

Both the administration and the student council made it difficult for us to get SOC official recognition by placing a number of procedural roadblocks in our way. Our first grievous "mistake" was our failure to draw up a proper constitution for the organization. Then, when the charter had passed both houses and had been signed by the Student Government president, we had to submit it again because it had not distinguished between the articles and the bylaws. *Silver Chips,* the school paper, quoted the Student Government president as saying that some members looked on SOC as "some sort of left-

ish organization out to cause trouble." Norm Solomon un-
earthed the fact that another group, the Model Rocketry Club,
had been quickly approved by the Student Government and
recognized by the school administration.

Finally we were officially approved after all this parliamen-
tary and procedural hassling. We quickly organized a series of
programs that enabled us to build a solid base of support
among the students. Our first program brought the Night-
hawk, a black disc jockey from the District, to Blair to ex-
pound on soul music. The gymnasium was filled to capacity.
Discussions on the "psychological hangups of teachers" (led by
a local psychiatrist), on Buddhism, and on the American right
followed.

But kids in the group wanted to do more than talk. Some of
them wanted to organize protests against the county regulations on leafleting and against the forthcoming military service
assembly. We wanted the assembly (at which representatives
from all the services spoke to the senior class) to include a discussion of alternatives to the draft. Yet SOC was not an effective vehicle for political action. We talked more than we acted.
We never were able to attract enough student support to carry
out a successful action, and most of our plans fizzled. We never
quite believed that we could make the slightest dent in the
way the administration ran the school. Our experience organizing SOC taught us that the administration would resist even
the most minor change in the status quo. Much of our energy
was sapped simply trying to survive from day to day. Many of
the kids got stoned just to get through their classes. I returned
home feeling physically exhausted from my struggles trying to
cope with that absurd universe. We expended so much energy
trying to stay on our feet that we had little left over for practical organization.

The talking we did together and the close personal ties that
began to develop between us helped to make SOC a community in an otherwise impersonal structure. We were free to get
to know each other without regulation from a classroom time-
table. Kids who had once felt awfully alone, who had person-
alized their problems, met others in the same situation. Free

from many of the standardized roles and superficial forms of communication we had previously been locked into, we began to analyze the educational system that had been repressing us. Together we tried to understand the function of public schools, to envision what learning would be like in a really free environment.

It was clear that SOC was not meeting all our needs, but we were not sure what would. One night in February Norm Solomon invited me to his home for dinner. Bill Higgs, an activist lawyer in D.C. who had defended James Meredith in Mississippi, and Larry Fishman, another Blair student, were also there. Jeremiah came over later in the evening. We were discussing life at Blair when Bill in a perfectly straightforward way asked us, "Why don't you guys start your own school?" Bill had a knack for making the most outlandish experiments seem easy—he was incurably optimistic. We all became very excited. When we told Jeremiah what we had been talking about he said, "Great, but all I ever hear is talk. Let's go ahead and do it." It was a perfectly outrageous idea that answered all our most immediate needs. That we hadn't thought of it ourselves was a measure of how constricted our vision had been. Blair was our universe—nothing else seemed quite real.

For the next several days and for weeks thereafter we talked lyrically about the free school. The students talked to their friends at Blair. I persuaded Ira Hirsch, a friend in Antioch-Putney who was teaching at the Adams-Morgan School, and Steve, with whom I shared an apartment, to join us. We had to keep convincing each other that our idea would become real, that it just wouldn't stay in the fantasy stage. We now had a chance to create our own school, an institution we could control and own. All our efforts to change conditions at Blair had been going nowhere, and we were becoming increasingly frustrated. We had no answers for those who asked us what alternative we had for the present system. Here was an opportunity to begin living what we had been preaching rather than waiting for utopia to come someday.

The kids at Blair who were attracted to the project and I had one thing in common. We were all bored. No common ideology, no common view of what our school's purpose should be, bound us together. The atmosphere at school was choking us to death and we wanted out. It was the atmosphere more than any specific acts of repression directed against us that made us leave; we were rebelling against a total environment.

One movement organizer in Washington, who later became a Weatherwoman, accused us of being utopian—as if this were a cardinal sin. She felt—and her position is shared by some segments of the left—that it was a cop-out for teachers and students to leave public schools. If students stayed locked in the jaws of Leviathan, their experience would radicalize them, which was to be desired. The proper role for radical teachers was to give political direction to the struggles that students would undertake.

Many radicals have endless discussions about whether it is better to work within established institutions or to create alternatives of one's own. But this was an academic issue to all of us. It was an abstract consideration compared to the acutely personal impulses we felt. We acted out of necessity—we had no other options. Greg, one of the kids most active in the project, told me later that if the school hadn't come along he would have hit the road for California. We were so uncomfortable where we were that it seemed useless to examine the correctness of our motives. It was only in the course of our day-to-day work in the school that we got a glimpse of the direction we might go in, the goals we might set for ourselves.

We used SOC as a base to find recruits for the school. We wrote up a leaflet analyzing the failures of the public schools and presenting our vision as an alternative to them which we circulated to students at Blair and at other schools in the District, in Maryland, and in Virginia. This decision was important, because we were consciously trying to reverse the normal pattern of starting a school—that is, by first appealing to parents. Since we wanted our school to be under the control of its students, they, we felt, were the ones we first had to convince of its validity. We also appeared on a radio talk show, placed an ad in the Washington *Free Press,* and spoke at meetings of high school students. Word spread through the underground grapevine that a free school was being born, and students and parents contacted us to find out about it.

But gaining new converts and keeping our morale up was difficult. When we described the project, we spun its outlines from our imagination. We had no building, no money, no definite curriculum—in short, none of the things that most people associated with a school. If a student was the slightest bit timid or conservative, he would not stay with us for long. I asked myself what I would do if the school never got off the ground. Should I have another job waiting in case we failed, should I keep my options open? I plunged ahead into the unknown and threw my anxieties to the wind. Organizing the school was helping me become a gutsier person.

The kids who were thinking of dropping out of public school faced even greater risks. They would be leaving the traditional route that led to college, career, and secure life style, and they had to buck their parents in the process. Many of the parents never quite believed that we would pull off the project and feared the worst for their kids' futures. In some cases they made us, the older people involved, the scapegoats for all the tensions that wracked their families. If their sons and daughters wanted to leave home, drop out of school, or just acquire more independence, we must have planted these subversive ideas in their heads.

When I look back on these anxious months I wonder why we kept with it. Most of us were adventurous types, had done things before they were fashionable, came from unusual backgrounds. Some of the kids had taken drugs before they became a fad, hitchhiked on their own, and had wrested a considerable amount of independence from their parents. Greg had hung out on the fringes of the Beat generation in Venice, California. He used to read free-form poetry and listen to jazz and jugband music. Kids whose older brothers were Beats first turned him on to grass when he was fourteen. Greg was excited by the existentialists—by Camus and Sartre—and had an intense interest in Zen and Eastern religions. He hitchhiked through the South when he was quite young. Jeremiah's parents were active in the Washington peace movement and were practicing vegetarians. Bill Higgs, a white Mississippian, rebelled against southern folk ways by defending the rights of James Meredith. Ira, who now was active in the project, had refused induction and had been placed on probation.

We had a series of biweekly meetings and picnics with interested students, parents, and teachers in the area, culminating in a spring retreat in the Shenandoahs. Roles of "teachers" and "students" that had previously obstructed communication began to break down in these informal settings. These meetings frequently resembled "self-criticism" sessions in which we tried to encourage each other to articulate what we felt was wrong about our schools and to suggest a concrete alternative to them. As we tried to fashion a common educational philosophy we became a more cohesive group. But surprisingly little in the way of concrete proposals or programs came out of them. This was natural, given the transient involvement of many of the people present. Except for a hard core of eight to ten kids plus myself, Steve, Ira, and Bill Higgs, the people attending the meetings changed from week to week. There was an air of unreality about the whole project. Only a handful seemed ready to commit themselves to it, and, since we lacked a building, we had great difficulty convincing the more hesitant people of our seriousness. When would we ever know, we asked ourselves, who was really with us?

One important thing came out of these meetings. We decided to orient the school toward white, middle-class students. Any illusions we might have had about an integrated effort were dispelled when we spoke to some very savvy black kids from Eastern High School in D.C. who came to one of our meetings. They said they liked what we were doing, but it was irrelevant to the kind of "freedom school" they wanted. They suggested that we complement and support each other, not try to duplicate each other's functions.

Our core group had in common a dissatisfaction with the public schools and, more fundamentally, with the patterns of coercive authority embodied in them. But we knew much more about what we didn't like about public school than what we wanted to erect in its place. We did have some general goals.

We wanted to break down the distinctions between teachers and students. This we hoped to do by renting communes in the District where students and teachers from the school would live and where many of our activities would take place. In this framework, we hoped, easy, natural association would break down many of the normal barriers and we would all begin to share in making decisions about the school. Our leaflet stated that "the learning process should be one in which we share our knowledge and experience. Education goes beyond the class-room and involves the whole person." We expressed our vision in lofty rhetoric, in phrases whose content still needed to be filled in.

We rarely anticipated any of the practical problems we were to face, though we did discuss how we should handle the use of drugs in the school. Our retreat in the Shenandoahs taught us how explosive an issue it could be. We sent out letters to all the parents inviting them to come along if they wished. We thought that this gesture would make our excursion legitimate and expected none of the adults to take us up on it. One man did decide to come along. His daughter, who was not really interested in the school, was friendly with one of the organizers of our project, a black student at Blair. Her father probably joined us to make sure our black friend did not molest his daughter.

This man turned out to be an amateur investigator of pri-vate schools, and used his time to muckrake the project. Many of the kids smoked grass, and none of the older people who came along objected. We felt that the kids should make their own decisions on using dope and that we would only hinder this process by acting as their moral guardians. As it turned out, a couple of the kids initiated a discussion of drugs during the retreat. As a result of the discussion the kids decided it would be unwise to use drugs at the school or during any of our activities.

After the weekend the girl's father called the wife of a prom-inent government official, whose daughter was on the retreat, to report on our nefarious activities. Did she know, he asked her, that kids were smoking grass and sleeping in the same tents and that the adults who came along encouraged these practices? The woman then called me to ask me if this was all true. I tried to defend what we had done in a long, anguished phone conversation. Since she was still upset, I suggested that the older people in the school come out to her home to talk about it. She invited us all out to her spacious Virginia home for dinner. Steve, Ira, Bill Higgs, a friend of Bill's, and I went. During dinner the woman raised the question of drugs on the retreat. Over and over again she kept saying, "You know I don't disapprove of drugs, but how could you boys be so indiscreet?" We finally were able to pacify her, to convince her that we were sane and responsible men. During the drive home we discovered that Bill's friend had been stoned throughout the entire evening.

Both the older and younger people shared equally in planning the project. None of the kids wanted us to be their "leaders" or "representatives." Anyone could act as spokesman at meetings, recruit new students, and carry out other necessary tasks. We tended to handle a lot more of the necessary administrative details (writing to colleges, checking legal requirements, and the like). But this did not alter the feeling that we were all in this together, that each of us had a say in determining the character of the school.

Before the school had formally begun, close ties of mutual trust and friendship bound us together. Had we simply bought a building, written up a curriculum, and then attracted students, the school would have been a much different place, a much less organic educational community. We all learned as much (and probably more) from the painful struggle of creating our own school as we did from any of the classes that we later organized. And what's more, each one of us had a vital, personal stake in the project. Since we were building it together, there was no one to blame for our mistakes. In public school we could always blame the administration for all our problems. Now the burden was on us, there were no easy copouts.

The close relationships we had with each other were like those that developed between northern college students and young southern blacks in the freedom schools organized in the South during the summer of 1964. There, too, the process of creating a school from scratch was as important as any formal classes that were held, and the style of the classes was substantially different, much less abstract and impersonal, because of it. Staughton Lynd captures the spirit of the Mississippi freedom schools, the project he directed for SNCC in 1964.

> There Northern white college students and Southern black teenagers had first to encounter one another as whole human beings, to establish trust. This happened in the process of finding a church basement together, deciding on a curriculum together, improvising materials together, that is, in the context of common work; and it matured in that context too, as those who walked together in the morning registered voters together in the afternoon. . . . What we read together in the mornings was often James Joyce, what was talked about may have been French or algebra as well as Negro history. But I simply testify that the context of shared experience (which meant, too, that teachers characteristically boarded in their students' homes) made all the difference *(Intellectuals, the University, and the Movement,* New England Free Press pamphlet).

Once they heard about the school, the Blair administration decided to make my life as uncomfortable as possible. Some parents had apparently called the school because their children were threatening to drop out of school to join us. Some of the teachers who taught "honors" classes felt threatened because some of their most creative students were talking about leaving high school. One of these students, Norman Solomon, had the best chance of becoming the next editor of the school paper. *Silver Chips* quoted the reactions of several other teachers to our project. One of the most progressive English teachers commented: "The school should not grow out of criticism of the public schools. It should be a supplement to public schools, not competition." Another teacher objected: "I don't see any math or science or language courses on the flyer." The eleventh-grade class adviser was concerned that "the free school has become a rationalization for not working and [for] dropping out." My team leader told me that other teachers felt that we were manipulating kids, encouraging them to leave high school without giving them an honest picture of the risks involved.

The liberal teachers at Blair were probably the most critical of the project. They resented the activist role I was playing in the school. Teachers, they felt, should confine themselves to developing more innovative methods of instruction. Their classrooms were the showcases of the school, the models of what was best in the "new social studies," the "new English." They had the chance to work with the most highly motivated students, with honor classes. The administration, I felt, permitted these teachers to experiment to their hearts content as long as they muffled their voices about the repressive atmosphere of the school. That was the unwritten agreement they had made, which I had broken.

The "dropout" problem was a highly charged issue at Blair, which the announcement of the "free school" had inflamed. In a full-page spread on dropouts *Silver Chips* stated that 110 students withdrew in 1966–67 and that 45 had left school as of April 1968. In 1966–67, 4.7 per cent of Blair's student body had dropped out of school, compared with 1.26 per cent in Montgomery County as a whole.

Things came to a head when the principal called me into his office in the spring ostensibly to talk about my teaching experiences that year. One of the directors of the Washington office of Antioch-Putney and my Blair supervisor were also present. The principal hinted that my work organizing the school might be in "conflict of interest" with my responsibilities as a teacher. He also cautioned me against using my classroom as a forum to proselytize the project. Neither my supervisor nor the representative from Antioch-Putney came to my support.

To make things more tense, the assistant principal came in halfway through the discussion to talk with the principal. He looked shocked. My team leader followed him into the office a few minutes later. The assistant principal had found two very scruffy-looking young men in blue work shirts carrying cameras and lighting equipment on their backs at the entrance to the school. His first reaction was that they were vandals who were unlawfully intruding on school property. When he challenged them he discovered that they were coming to perform a light show in my fourth-period American history class. I had asked them to come several days before but had forgotten to secure official permission. This was what the uproar was all about. The principal sent another one of the assistant principals in to observe the class. I stayed in the principal's office for the rest of the interrogation and missed the light show and the Marshall McLuhan record that accompanied it.

The principal left the question of "conflict of interest" up in the air. This would scare me more, he may have calculated, than if he made a definitive judgment on it. He said that he would talk with the central office in Rockville to determine whether I was acting in conflict with Board regulations. If he ever got a ruling from the central office, I never heard about it. But he succeeded in making my days as anxious, as suspense-filled, as possible. I never knew from one day to the next whether I would be fired or not.

When we circulated our leaflet at Blair, the principal tried to squelch our campaign. He called me into his office to tell me that it was customary to get school approval before handing out leaflets. I told him that this policy violated the right to free speech. He made no response. Since we had already circulated a good number of leaflets, he said, there was little he could do. But he did succeed in intimidating us and preventing us from handing out leaflets after this—at least on a large-scale, wide-open basis. We were reluctant to confront the county's anti-leafleting regulations. We already had enough hassles just organizing the school without adding on any more burdens.

As I look back on all of this now, I realize how powerful the weapon against free circulation of leaflets and other public notices is in the hands of the administration. By allowing the public school bureaucracy to define what acceptable speech and opinion is, these regulations may easily cripple the efforts of parents, teachers, and students to form educational alternatives. They certainly took a lot of the steam out of our organizing.

Throughout the year the administration had been disturbed by my unorthodox classroom practices. Once the principal called me into his office to ask me if I would submit a report on my progress in my American history class. "About this time of year," he said, "we usually are up to Reconstruction." He knew quite well that I had discarded the textbook early in the year. On another occasion he asked me if I wouldn't mind if someone from the administration sat in when Bill Higgs came to talk to my history class. I flatly refused. An assistant principal once walked into my classroom to find a small group of students listening to Bob Dylan's "Subterranean Homesick Blues." I had left the classroom for a few moments. "Where's the teacher, where's the class?" she exclaimed. One of the students responded, "It's right here." They were so disturbed by my failure to require students to attend class that during the last week or two of school a loudspeaker announcement blared, "Will Mr. Denker's students please come to his fourth-period class for the rest of the year."

The administration also came down hard on some of the SOC kids when they organized antiwar actions at the time of the student strike. Jeremiah, Greg, and Judy, three of the students most active in planning the school, and some of their friends dreamed up a leaflet that called for napalming a dog on April 26, the day of the International Student Strike. When Jeremiah showed the leaflets to students in my American history class, some of them got incensed that he could plan such an inhuman act. Jeremiah asked them how they could quietly accept the murder of civilians in Vietnam. One of the girls threatened to have her father call the SPCA. It was one of the most alive classes I had all year. As the leaflets circulated through the building, rumors spread that the "greasers" in the school would face down the "hippies" if they tried to carry out their plans. The County Humane Society called the school to protest. Finally the administration suspended Jeremiah, Greg, and four other students for leafleting without permission.

When Jeremiah came to school at 7:30 the next morning with three signs to picket against the war, the principal had the county police arrest him on his lone vigil. A police car followed him and his mother from their home to the school. He was charged with breach of the peace and suspended from school for a week. He was marching on the same spot where, several months before, Blair teachers had picketed during a strike for higher wages. The word among a number of the faculty was that I had put him up to it. Later the administration told him that he could not come on school property and threatened him with arrest if he did. The principal was so anxious to prevent him from inciting other students that he permitted him to do his course work at home.

In the meantime we had been working on the administrative chores that had to be completed if the school was to begin by the end of summer. Parents and their kids often asked us if colleges would accept students graduating from an unaccredited, free-form school. Most people assumed that going to a bizarre experiment like ours would close out all their options. We asked ourselves many times if we weren't compromising the project by trying to make it acceptable to colleges. But since we felt we had to allay the fears of our prospective students, we decided to write letters to a group of colleges about our project. We wrote to some small progressive colleges (Antioch, Goddard, Reed), but also to Yale, Wesleyan, and the University of Chicago. Their responses were positive. On the basis of their letters we decided that we would send a rather unconventional "transcript" to colleges students wanted to apply to. A student would prepare a portfolio that might include samples of his work, a running log of learning experiences, accounts of his classes. Teachers would submit recommendations.

We spent a lot of time talking with the parents of the kids who wanted to go to the school. But if the kids had not tried to persuade their parents that they were really serious, that they had no intention of returning to public school, our arguments would have had little effect. At best we provided reinforcement for decisions that were resolved in a struggle between parents and their sons or daughters. We did give the project a legitimacy, an aura of respectability, in the eyes of the parents.

We were so eager, though, to win their support that we tried to sell the free school to them. We made our project appear to be much more organized than it really was. We minimized our legal hassles and financial difficulties. We portrayed the school as if we already had developed a program and had found sufficient resource people to work with our students.

We had gone ahead from the very beginning, blissfully ignorant of the laws and regulations that would affect our status as a school in the District. It was not until late June that Ira and I sat down with Alex Rode, who had run an early experimental school in D.C., to find out about our probable legal hassles. Since Washington had no formal accreditation agency, Alex said, the zoning board would probably confront us with our real problems. The law required schools to be located in a commercially zoned area, not in a residential community. The late-nineteenth-century codes stipulated that a school building had to have steel doors, fire escapes, stairwells, a parking space for each teacher regardless of whether he had a car. Since we had little or no money, we could not afford the renovating costs that an operation like this would demand. The zoning department had closed down Alex's school and once had had him hauled off to court as if he were a child molester. We talked about trying to find a local church (which would pass zoning regulations) that would serve as our official headquarters and mailing address. Once we had secured our "cover," we would have most of our classes and activities in the communes. This cover, we hoped, would protect us from harassment by the city.

Steve, Ira, and I left Washington for Vermont in late June to spend a month finishing up the requirements for the master's degree. A number of the kids were scattering and were planning to return in August. Only a few of them had made absolute commitments to join the project in September. A small group of students, a girl from Antioch, and Bill Higgs were staying in Washington to finish the remaining organizational work. When we left for Vermont the school was still much more a creation of our imagination than any kind of concrete reality.

CHAPTER III

Joel: The First Year

1. *Getting Started*

The last weeks in Washington had been incredibly hectic, the weather humid and swampy. I was exhausted. Leaving the city required an act of faith—so many things were left undone. The school, I hoped, would magically pull itself together by the fall.

Alex's news had left me in a state of shock. I was sure the zoning board would close us down as soon as we started. I also felt that none of our ruses would fool them. Would we be able to find a house? If we did, where would we get the money to rent it? Would the kids cop out at the last minute? Would we? I couldn't really enjoy the Vermont hills when my mind was many miles away.

We were no longer public school teachers; Ira had left Morgan Community, Steve, McKinley High School, and I Montgomery Blair. It would be impossible in our project to hide behind our professional roles—our blemishes would be there for everyone to see. I don't think any one of us was sure how he would meet the test of honest, personal encounter in a school community.

In our respective schools we each had been a gadfly. We were always carping, complaining about the "system," about the weaknesses of our fellow teachers. It was easy enough to damn

74

the public schools. But could we, as Steve put it that summer, "channel our rebellious and nihilistic energies into a concrete project"?

That summer a new teacher joined our group. Arthur Berg was a friend of Ira's who had recently returned from Israel. He was a very gifted student of science. Ira and I talked lyrically about the school when he came to visit us in Vermont. Instead of honestly presenting the strengths and weaknesses of our project, we tried to sell it to him. Arthur would not have the chance to test our rhetoric until he arrived in Washington in late August.

Our sole contacts with Washington that summer were several phone calls to Joan Trey, a wonderfully hard-working Antioch student who had agreed to take care of the administrative work in our absence. But summer, we were learning, was a difficult time to organize a project. Many of the most active kids were away, and those who remained had their minds on other things. September and the opening of public schools was still far away. For those still uncommitted to the school it was a remote and abstract alternative.

When we came back from Vermont in early August we still hadn't found a house. If we didn't find one soon, no one would take our project seriously. Ira and I and a few of the kids— Greg, Judy, and Norman—began scouring the low-rent areas of D.C. for a house that would be suitable for a commune of eight to ten persons. We read the ads in the *Post* and the *Star* every day.

We were incredibly innocent. None of us knew how to deal with landlords or real estate agents. We didn't know whether to be really honest about our plans or to put up a clever front. If the landlords knew the truth, they certainly wouldn't rent to a band of longhairs. If we lied, they would find out sooner or later and we'd be out on the streets again. Sometimes we lied, sometimes we told the truth, but neither method seemed to work. Ira and I did most of the talking. We figured that landlords would rather talk to "adults," even shaggy ones, than to a bunch of freaky high school kids. Also, the law prevented anyone under eighteen from signing a lease.

Once Ira and I went to one of Washington's biggest slum-lords to ask about a house we had seen in the Dupont Circle area. The place was just splendid—it had more than enough bedrooms, rooms for meeting, a large basement. The woman at the firm handed us a form—the respectability test. We had to prove we were employed, financially solvent, and men of character. Ira wrote on the form that he had been convicted of a felony—draft refusal. We also listed the names and ages of the kids who expected to live there. We never got the house.

While we were searching for a house we also had to complete other last-minute chores. For example, we had to charter the project as a nonprofit corporation. Getting nonprofit status was the first step toward becoming a tax-exempt organization. Bill Higgs, who would soon leave Washington to become legal adviser to Reies Tijerina in New Mexico, had written up our articles of incorporation. We named officers and directors, both young and old, and one hot day carried our papers over to a liquor store to have them notarized. We then brought them over to the Recorder of Deeds.

If we did not outwardly appear a tightly knit organization, at least on paper we attained full respectability. "The purpose of the corporation [we called ourselves the New Educational Project Inc.] is to carry on general educational research and activities, in particular to provide for the education of children at the junior high and high school levels. The corporation will also attempt to do experimental research in the most effective way of educating children of different racial and economic backgrounds."

After two weeks of searching we still hadn't found a house. One evening Ira and I spotted an ad in the *Star* for a house on Madison Street. At this point we were ready to take anything. Arthur, Ira, and I put on coats and ties and went off into the humid night. We discovered that Madison Street was located on the upper part of Sixteenth Street, an integrated middle-class neighborhood of single-family, detached homes with neat, well-kept lawns.

We met our prospective landlord, Mr. Patel, and his brother, both polished Indian gentlemen. Mr. Patel was a financial officer at the Indian Embassy and his brother was a professor of law at a Canadian university. Patel also speculated in real estate—he owned some houses and apartments in D.C. We told them we were teachers and that we operated a school in another part of Washington.

They were impressed with us. Later Patel remarked that I looked very English. We were young bachelors—in their eyes ideal tenants for the house. Patel himself had lived in the house with some other young men before he was married. Our rambling, leisurely conversation with them was more a character test than anything else. Patel kept business matters in the background. It was a parody of an English tearoom, but with two Anglo-Indians presiding.

At last Patel told us that he would rent the house to us. We gave him all the money we had and told him we would bring the rest of the deposit the next day. We departed, elated that our seemingly fruitless search had ended. We rationalized any doubts we had about the landlord and the neighborhood and suppressed the fear that we might get caught when the kids moved in. In order to pay the landlord we borrowed money, used our own savings, and got contributions from Norman and Judy.

With the rental of the house on Madison Street the project was at last acquiring some substance. People who once thought that our plans to create a school were merely wishful thinking, a fantasy, realized that we were serious. Kids began to make the anxious decision to drop out of school, parents began to loosen their grip. Bill Higgs had been right when he said that most kids would not decide to go to the school until the last moment, when they were faced with the immediate problem of whether or not to go back to public high school.

We quickly began the move into Madison Street. There would be as many as twelve people living there during the next two months: Ira, Arthur, Steve, Bill Howe (a friend of ours from Antioch-Putney who was teaching in a junior high school in the District), myself, Judy (17), from Montgomery Blair, Charlie (18), a Blair dropout, Audrey, his girl friend, Sam (12), Kathy (15), Alice (16), and Greg (17), also from

Blair. There were another fifteen kids, not living at the house, who would be involved full time in the school that fall.

Even after we had found a house and had all moved in, our problems were not over. We needed to find a place in which we could legally hold classes, an official address for the New Educational Project. We had been looking for a friendly church that we could use since we had gotten back from Vermont. We were afraid that if we didn't find one soon, the zoning inspectors would close us down.

We got to know a sympathetic minister at a Unitarian church in the District that was a few blocks from the Cardozo ghetto. He was all for having us use his church, but he had to get his board's approval. His board was made up of predominantly white middle-class folk and a token number of blacks. Arthur and I spoke to this group several times, giving them the pitch we generally gave an audience of respectable people. We tried to sell the school as a solid, serious educational experiment. But some of the board members still had misgivings about our politics, our participation in the antiwar movement, and our philosophy of education. The board kept procrastinating.

Arthur and I also talked with one of the directors of the Antioch-Putney Graduate program about giving us space. The director, who had been my supervisor at Blair, said that they had plans to use their basement for a recreation room for the graduate students—that is, a beer hall.

Since the church had postponed making a decision, we would not have a legal address for the project by the time that public schools opened in early September. We worried about how we were going to protect ourselves against the certain arrival of zoning inspectors and truant officers. We were much more security-conscious than the kids were—our paranoia knew no bounds. With no legal quarters, we began classes in our house and in Rock Creek Park. I remember having a discussion on the Book of Job and thinking that a group of well-dressed men walking by were plainclothes detectives.

We even feared that letters sent to Madison Street bearing

the name of the school would give away our identity to the authorities. To guard against this, Arthur and I went down to the post office to see if we could get a box for all our official correspondence. But it would take several weeks to process our application. We decided to take our chances, to continue receiving mail at the Madison Street address. Arthur was finally able to persuade the Friends' Meeting House of Washington to sponsor our project, but the final decision didn't come until the middle of October.

While we were taking care of organizational business, I thought it would be exciting to organize a public meeting on the events at the Chicago Convention. This would help us break out of our isolation and make the Washington Free Community—the network of communes, radical professionals and street people—aware of our project. I invited three people to talk; a woman in SDS who had been involved in the street action, a writer friend of mine who was beaten up during the demonstrations, and a radical member of the Washington, D.C., delegation. The evening began with a huge spaghetti dinner at our new house. Some kids had arrived as early as five o'clock. By nine our house was jammed. There must have been about sixty people sitting on the floor and standing in both the living room and dining room.

The three speakers gave very different perspectives on Chicago. The woman spoke lyrically of fighting in the street, of resisting the police, of learning how to overcome passivity. She was excited that so many "greasers" had come out for the demonstrations. The young writer was shocked by the relentless brutality of the cops, by their contempt for students. (As they clubbed kids, some of them would scream "you rich bastards.") The woman criticized him for expressing shock. Shock, she said, was a luxury that white radicals could no longer afford— blacks had known the oppression of the police for years. White people should purge themselves of their idealism, of their illusions about society.

The Democratic delegate described how the Democratic party and the Daley machine had rigged the convention. The violence and repression outside had its counterpart in the gagging of free speech inside the convention hall, in the abuse the delegates suffered from the police and Daley hacks.

After their talks a woman from D.C. spoke about the warm feeling she had gotten from the white working-class kids whom she and her girl friend had met at the airport. But a young kid from Chicago, who had been a member of a gang there and had been busted several times, said that the "greasers" were not serious, that they were just hustling the radicals. A friend of mine, a southerner who had been active in the civil rights movement for several years, commented sardonically that the movement had "discovered" a new constituency. The meeting went on until late in the night. I notice that many of the kids in the school were filtering outside. They had grown bored with the political raps that older "new lefties" were into.

Since most of us had never lived in a commune before, we spent the first few months getting to know each other (staying up late, talking, going to the park, listening to music). It was sometimes difficult for me to share things with the kids, because I was not heavily involved with drugs. Many of the kids in the school had been doing drugs through most of their high school years. I had gotten into dope only after I had graduated from college. I was a beer drinker—a logical recreation for a student at a one-sex college in the mid-sixties. Alcohol and psychedelic drugs were worlds apart. Booze stimulated violent outbursts of energy, acid induced a quiet, passive state. When Greg, Charlie, and I went drinking, we found common ground. All of us liked to drink beer, to rap, laugh, kid each other.

Before beginning classes in mid-September we talked with most of the kids about the interests they wanted to pursue. Since in many cases we had already known each other for several months, we had a pretty easy time figuring out topics for classes. The first classes that emerged were a blend of the interests of the younger and older people. We had groups going in nonverbal communication (sensitivity training), rock music, literature, drama, psychology, poetry, philosophy, and African history. Arthur set up apprenticeships for Greg, Judy, and Alice with a metal sculptor, potter, and sculptor. Each group was made up of six to ten people and usually met twice a week. We still associated schedules with public school and consequently never set up one of our own till early in October. We usually met in our house or in Rock Creek Park.

Steve recalled one of those first classes.

> On a beautiful fall day we went to Rock Creek Park as part of what I called a "non-verbal communications" class. We found a large green field and sat for a while, just looking and listening. We stood up, joined hands, and formed a circle. Someone volunteered to be in the middle, and we passed him around the circle from person to person. Then we let him fall almost to the ground, lifted him up and gently rocked him back and forth. Slowly, we lowered him to the ground.
>
> After a while, I handed out the blindfolds I had prepared earlier. All of us put the blindfolds on and ran around dizzily, holding each other's hands. Again we lifted people, this time blindfolded, and dug the difference in the sensation. Finally, we formed a wide circle, got on hands and knees and began crawling blindly toward each other. Sometimes, we had to crawl over each other, sometimes we completely missed, mostly we laughed.

But the classes did not set the tone of our community. Writing poetry, art, playing and listening to music, had more personal urgency and produced more immediate, tangible results. Sometimes, when we tried to formalize a sensuous experience, we failed miserably. Steve and Larry Aaronson, a friend of ours teaching at a D.C. high school, hoped to do a course on rock music. After spending an evening discussing "Hey Jude" and "Revolution," by the Beatles, they realized no one was listening. Wisely they stopped the discussion, put on more music, and spent the rest of the night watching the fireplace.

Our best "classes" were frequently trips we took together. Several of us were reading *Marat/Sade* in a class I had organized on utopianism. The film came to the Biograph Theater, and a group of us decided to go. We were dazed by the brilliant portrayal of the inmates of an asylum enacting the madness and violence of the French Revolution. A girl who went with us had made brownies. After the movie we all plopped down in the middle of the theater lobby to eat them. Another time several of us went to hear a friend testify at a city council meeting on police repression only to hear the issue shelved and the more urgent topic of civilian escorts for funeral processions discussed.

The most powerful community experience that we participated in was our weekend trips to the Shenandoah Mountains. Arthur had met an architect named Roy Mason, who owned fifty acres near the site of an old mission on the top of a mountain in the Shenandoahs which he offered to let us use whenever we wanted.

We were always more relaxed and quiet in the mountains. Looking at the Japanese-like landscape, hiking in the woods, cooking meals, and talking together helped us feel quite close. Jeremiah and Larry, his traveling companion, talked about trying to survive at the mission throughout the winter. Other people would later talk about helping Roy to construct houses there. The times we had up at the mission became a kind of spiritual reference point against which we measured all the rest of our experiences.

The kids at the school also needed time to themselves—it was hard to keep sane otherwise. They wanted to distinguish their own needs from those their elders had instilled in them. The whole school experience was shaking up the way we all thought of ourselves and would certainly affect the kind of lives we would be living five or ten years hence.

Greg, one of the most creative kids living at Madison Street, had been taking drugs—grass, hash, acid—for a long time before he became involved with the school. During some periods he took acid every day. When the school began in September he decided to stop tripping. He now wanted to think about the "heavy" things he had discovered about himself as the result of doing drugs. He wanted to examine the relationship between his ego and the universe, a question that became important to him because of drugs and his interest in eastern religion. He also wanted to work out his hangups about authority. His art work—constructing metal sculpture—became a way of giving coherent expression to his turbulent feelings.

2. Confronting Outside Authorities

Living together also strengthened our sense of rightness—we enjoyed flouting authority, broadcasting our newly found life style and cohesiveness. One afternoon a group from the school were wading in Rock Creek Park. A mounted cop came by and ordered them out. When they finally did come out he informed them that it was against the law to be in the creek.

"How come?" they wanted to know.

"Because it's polluted," he answered.

"Well," Charlie suggested, "maybe the law should be against polluting the creek instead."

We also tended to view many of the parents as our enemies. Our feelings were reinforced when Judy's father tried to remove her from the school. Steve was intimately involved in that conflict.

> Judy spent all day Saturday morning nervously cleaning the house. Her father, who had been divorced and had since remarried, was coming with his new wife to visit. Most people spent the next morning at Sam's parents' house for breakfast and the afternoon at a free concert at the University of Maryland. When they returned, the house was in a turmoil. Judy had run away. Her parents were calling periodically to see if we knew where she was. Charlie explained that Judy's father had decided to remove her from the school. While she was supposedly removing her things from her room, Judy sneaked out the back door. Charlie lowered her stuff out of the window.
>
> She went to stay with a friend of ours downtown, but we didn't know that. Her parents came over. They had notified the police, who suggested we had something to do with her disappearance. Arthur, Ira, and I tried to talk with them, to find out why they wanted to remove her from the school.
>
> Judy's father was the spokesman. "This situation is too unstructured for Judy. I'm a psychologist, you know—I've seen many cases like her. She needs some firm and definite limits. Her mother is not a strong person. She let Judy go here against her better judgment."
>
> Judy's mother sat through this silently.

"Don't you know how important it is for her to live here?" Arthur asked. "If it weren't important, why would she have tried to run away?"

"She doesn't *know* what she wants. She's very confused. Who knows where she is or whether she's alive or not?" her mother asked.

We told them she was all right.

"Do you know where she is?"

"No, we don't. But we're positive she'll get in touch with us. [She had, in fact, called while we were talking.] If you want to show her that you are ready to talk with her," Arthur said, "then tell the police that she's all right, to stop looking for her. It could really be an ugly scene if they found her before we did."

Reluctantly Judy's father called the police—they made some remark, warning them about hippie-Commies. Arthur and I drove downtown to pick Judy up. She confronted her parents uneasily. Once again we went upstairs to talk. Judy told her father how much she felt a part of the house, how she was taking responsibility on her own. No one was judging her. She had begun to feel comfortable.

Her parents realized she was serious. As a "compromise" Judy would stay with her mother and spend the rest of the time at the school. The meeting lasted hours. None of us had eaten. When the issue was resolved, Judy's parents went out and bought us some hamburgers and milkshakes. All of us felt grateful that it was over. The next day a cop came by looking for Judy. I explained that she had returned with her parents. Apparently the police didn't trust them either.

We were anxious about our visibility in the neighborhood. The elderly people who lived on either side of us had a perfect view of our activities. The sight of long-haired freaks lounging on the front steps or walking down the quiet street was certain to frighten people on the block. Sometimes it seemed as if no one but us lived on Madison Street—people stayed inside their homes and emerged occasionally to water their lawns or wash their cars.

Our neighbors must have looked on us as a strange and alien tribe that might corrupt the minds of their sons and daughters. They had all kinds of fantasies, I'm sure, about what we were doing in the house. I doubt, though, that they ever imagined we were running a school.

We made a few feeble gestures to identify with the community. Bill Howe suggested that our place be reasonably well kept, that we rake the leaves, mow the lawn, and water the grass. But most of us had difficulty acting like proper suburban citizens. And even if we had kept our place immaculate, I am not sure our neighbors would have accepted us—our attitudes and theirs were worlds apart.

Bill Howe once overheard a conversation between the man across the street and a local cop. They were chatting in quite a jovial manner. Our neighbor asked him if he could get him the correct information on how to register his gun. People on our block viewed the police as their protection against criminals and other disorderly elements. We tended to look on the police as an immediate threat to our security, even when there was no rational basis for our fears.

One morning Patel came over to the house to tell us that the FBI had been talking to some neighbors about us. They, in turn, had called him. The presence of the FBI intensified suspicions they already had. One of our neighbors later told Patel that she had seen a guy and a girl playing a guitar together on the back porch late at night. After playing a guitar, what would they do next?

Patel had a brilliant way of masking his emotions. He looked the unruffled aristocrat who had come by to look over his property. Beneath his façade I am sure he was troubled. For in his eyes we had broken a gentleman's agreement. We were not the men of character he had imagined us, nor were we living the quiet, serene life he had expected us, as scholars, to be accustomed to. He later told me a long, involved fable— which I have long since forgotten—whose lesson was the virtues of a leisurely existence, a life unmarred by the strumming of guitars, of loud stereos. He also was upset because we threatened his precarious political status—he had his house insured with the State Department and was applying for American citizenship.

Patel's revelation about the Feds shocked me. I wondered

how long it would be before they came knocking on our door. We realized how naïve we were to think that we could fool our landlord and our neighbors, to make them think that no kids were living at our house. Being persecuted, however, raised our morale. We were pure; all of the devils were on the other side.

We never found out for sure exactly how the FBI got on our trail. Since Washington is a federal town, Hoover's boys get into almost anything that looks deviant. Perhaps our phone was tapped—a reasonable assumption for any movement group to make. Maybe our Chicago meeting aroused the suspicion of the authorities. Also, two kids who had been arrested for selling grass to an agent had been frequenting the school. All of these speculations may be beside the point. The students at Madison Street were young, living away from home, outside the public schools. That's subversive enough these days.

The FBI helped us to make our first policy decision, a rule on the use of drugs in the house. Ever since we began organizing the school we had known that we would have to make a decision on whether or not we would allow drugs in our school. Parents always asked us about our own attitude toward drugs and about what the school policy was on them. We told them that "we" were not the "school," that all rules would have to be decided by everyone involved. If the kids associated a rule on drugs with our whims, they would never obey it.

Now the issue was no longer academic. One night, before the FBI had come, we all sat down after dinner to talk about it. Ira and Arthur suggested that we allow drugs to be used in the house but not stored there. I was very upset by what they said —I was sure that this lukewarm approach would never work. I said that we ought to banish drugs completely from Madison Street. I could not continue working in the school, I said, if we had an open-door policy on drugs—it was just too risky. At the end of the meeting we decided to ban drugs temporarily. When we heard about the FBI we made our decision final.

Greg, who had been using drugs since he was about fourteen, also felt very strongly about their being used in the school. Several of his friends had been busted, and one had been shot by a cop. Once a young guy from Runaway House who was a speed freak came out to visit the school. Some people in the school thought we should allow him to join the project despite this. But Greg was adamant—he had seen what speed does to the heads of those who used it and didn't want him to join us.

If we weren't paranoid enough at this point, we received some more news that confirmed the danger to our community. The mother of one of the girls in the school, whose husband was a high government official—our one link to the Establishment—called me to report two anonymous phone calls she had received, one from a young man claiming to know her daughter, the other from an older man using the White House line. The young man informed her that her daughter was using pot at a house the woman assumed was the school. The White House call contained a veiled threat. The man reported that the police were watching closely the house at which her daughter was supposedly using drugs; he implied she should withdraw her daughter from the school. The woman said she had no intention of taking her out of the school. Her parents' refusal to bow to intimidation may have been our best insurance against getting busted.

When he began to see that we weren't keeping our end of the bargain, Patel cleverly insisted on a month-to-month lease. In addition, he made various stipulations about our remaining there. He told us we would have to pay additional rent for each person above the five we had originally agreed would live there. We were already paying $275 a month. Eighty dollars additional would be more than we could afford. We told Patel we would move out within a month—by the middle of October. We were all discouraged that we would have to channel our energies into another frustrating search for a house and more rounds of negotiations with real estate agents.

One day a group of us—Steve and I and eight of the kids in the school—went looking for houses in the Columbia Road area, a predominantly black and Spanish community with a sizable minority of lower-income whites. We stopped at a real estate agency that controls many homes in the area. Steve and I went inside and the kids sat out on the steps. (We thought we'd have a better chance of renting the place if we went in alone.) When the Spanish owner came back he was disturbed to find our kids on his doorstep. He started shouting, shooing them as if they were so many flies who defiled his property. He threatened to call the police if they didn't leave.

After several weeks of searching, Randy Shaw (who was a teacher at Hamilton Junior High School in the District and taught drama in the school) and I found a house for rent in the Mount Pleasant area. Once a fashionable neighborhood for upper-middle-class people in Washington, the area contained large row houses with nice and sometimes spacious lawns. A large number of blacks and Spanish-speaking people had moved into the area in recent years. Its main street was like many ghetto blocks: the usual bars (Pancho's, the Raven Grill, the Crosstown), liquor stores, small food stores, and places selling sharp clothes. Unemployed black men walked the street or just sat on the stoops. Police cars prowled the streets at all times of the day or night. There was usually one parked in front of a bar that had frequent brawls.

Many whites still lived in Mount Pleasant. College students and people who wanted to start communes came there in search of cheap rents. A small colony of Appalachians also lived there. Older men and women, who had been left behind as their friends moved to more expensive areas in the city and the suburbs, lived in small rooming houses. You would see them sitting on the benches in the small square near the bus stop. Some middle-class and even wealthier people insisted on remaining in the area in spite of the decay and the rising crime rate.

The house we found was a three-story row house on Park Road, quite close to Rock Creek Park. Randy and I went to talk to the landlord. This time we were completely honest. We told him that we were working in a school and that young high-school-age kids would be living at the house. The landlord's only concern was that the kids be properly "supervised." We promised that they would be—what else could we say? The lease permitted eleven people to live in the house. Everyone was delighted about our find, and we began moving our be-

longings in a day short of the deadline Patel had set. We still
had lingering fears that the police and FBI were out to destroy
us. We had a great sense of our own importance.

Soon after we moved into Park Road, Bill Howe and Steve
were lounging around the dining room when the landlord, a
tall, well-dressed man, came by. We had not yet signed the
lease and he wanted to take care of this bit of business quickly.
"Is Mr. Denker here?" he asked.

I was at Randy Shaw's place a few blocks away. Steve asked
Bill to pick me up. Bill went off on his motorcycle, but after
forty-five minutes had passed he still had not returned. The
landlord was getting fidgety. Just then the phone rang. It was
Ira. "What's this I hear about an FBI agent at our house?"

Slowly we pieced it together. Bill, who had never met the
landlord, was put off by the distinguished-looking stranger and
concluded that he was from the FBI. He must have assumed
that Steve's request was code language for "Hide Joel!"

3. *Internal Conflicts*

In the previous two months our attentions had been turned
outward to the dangers posed by the FBI, the police, and our
neighbors. The struggles of the next three months grew out of
the mundane problems that emerge when younger and older
people with different life styles decide to live together. What
we had hoped would be an experiment in communal living to
bring us closer together instead polarized the group.

We often talked about the virtues of communal living, but
we rarely mentioned the practical problems that it involved.
Who would buy the food, who would prepare it, who would
clean up after meals? How would we go about cleaning the
house? How would we make sure that we had enough money
each month to pay for our rent and food? How would we divide the costs between us? Should we set a limit on the number
of people who could eat their meals at the house? Should we
permit people to crash there?

Many of the kids who lived at Park Road and in the apartment at Lamont Street (where Randy and I stayed) did not want to set up any kind of structure—whether a daily schedule or regular meetings—to tackle these problems. They associated structure with being coerced or manipulated. Being free was being left alone, not being hassled. Whenever anyone—and it was usually one of the "adults" living at the house—suggested a schedule for dividing the work he was called "authoritarian."

The house had become increasingly messy, and we had begun to have house meetings to deal with it.

"I think what we need is a cooking and cleaning schedule. Everyone should take turns doing the shitwork," Arthur suggested.

Dave became enraged. "Nobody's going to make me do dishes at eight in the morning!"

"Nobody *is,* man!" Steve said. "We're not going to ask the unreal or impossible from you. This will make it easier for everyone."

Dave: "Well, I still think a schedule interferes with my freedom."

Steve: "What about the freedom of the people who get left with the work?"

We voted to try a schedule for a week; Dave abstained.

No schedule lasted for more than a week. Many kids felt that work should be done spontaneously whenever anyone saw a job that needed to be done. One of the kids told a reporter later in the year: "There were a lot of dirty dishes in the kitchen the other night and I couldn't stand it any more. So I started washing them and someone came along and said 'Oh, you're doing dishes,' and began to dry them. Then somebody else swept the floor."

Since we had no effective mechanism for making decisions in the school, each person had to act alone—he could expect no support from anyone else. If someone took real initiative (by asking a "crasher" to leave, for example), others might label him an "authoritarian motherfucker."

Even the older people argued about how much structure the

house should have. Randy Shaw was the unofficial leader of the "anarchist" contingent in our community. Steve was later to say Randy was the most authoritarian anarchist he had ever met. Randy relished leading mutinies against the schedules we periodically set up. A bundle of contradictions, he was probably the most compassionate person in the school. He was always willing to drive people around in his VW bus, to board people in his small apartment, and to contribute money whenever it was needed. Randy was not opposed to doing work around the house, but he wanted to do it when he felt like it. "I like garbage," Randy said. "If you don't like it, you can get rid of it."

"Suppose garbage makes me uptight—and we have to live together?" Steve asked.

"That's tough," Randy replied. "That's your hangup."

Yet, a few days later, Randy spontaneously washed and waxed the dining-room floor.

Arthur, the person who most frequently called for more structure at Park Road, was an enigmatic figure. He had an overwhelming concern for the well-being of the kids. When Charlie and Audrey, a couple living at the house, had a fight and Audrey left, Arthur stayed up most of the night talking with Charlie, comforting him. When Judy ran away, Arthur worked hardest to convince her parents that the school was best for her. He led excursions to swim at the Potomac, to watch clouds at Rock Creek Park. Nevertheless all of his concern had a price. Since he instinctively did things out of love, he expected others to act in the same way. He tried to convince kids that doing household chores—like washing dishes or cooking—was a way of expressing love. Many of them resented it when Arthur challenged them for acting irresponsibly.

Money was a source of constant tension between the older and younger people in the house. Kids who could afford it contributed $75 a month for rent and food, and an additional "tuition" of $275–$350 if it didn't impose a burden on them. (The school provided room and board and a subsistence wage for teachers.) But some of the kids living in the house had no financial support from their families and therefore contributed no money toward rent and food. In effect, they lived there on the largesse of the parents who did give money to the school. Arthur didn't think this was fair. He saw paying as synonymous with concern for the community. At one meeting he and Ira confronted Charlie and Audrey with: "I can't understand why you aren't paying—you are working, Audrey."

"I'm working to pay off some old debts," she answered.

"What about you, Charlie? Why aren't you working?"

"Just because my parents can't pay, why should I be penalized?" he asked.

"Charlie, I don't think you care about the community," Arthur said.

Charlie and Audrey and some of the others present interpreted what Arthur said to mean: If you really love *me*, you'll pay rent.

Arthur and the other adults living at Park Road had many other gripes. The house was noisy. It was impossible for the older people to keep any stable sleeping schedule, to organize their classes in a quiet and relaxed way. There were always people visiting and others who used the house to crash for the night. Things were so transient that it was impossible to predict how many people would be eating dinner. There was always some new face at the dining room table, which sometimes seated as many as twenty people.

We quickly used up our monthly allowance for food. Later in the year the house had to eat oatmeal for two weeks because people had eaten up all the rest of the food. And since there was no schedule for preparing meals, people tended to have snacks at all times of the day and night. This only made our financial problems worse. Alice complained because much of the housework and preparation of meals seemed to fall on her shoulders.

Aside from the physical chaos, Arthur felt that many kids were unequipped to deal with the emotional disorder of our household. Judy, who had helped found the school, still had a difficult time making demands on people. Steve remembers one traumatic experience with her.

Soon after she moved in, Judy went out to sleep on the sun porch. I noticed that there wasn't a mattress up there. "Should I get you a mattress?" I asked.

"It's all right," she said. "I can do without one."

I got her the mattress anyway. "You don't have to be a martyr around here."

About a week later she told me that she appreciated the mattress.

Shortly before Judy was to spend Thanksgiving with her father in Baltimore she suddenly began to throw things around her room. Bill Howe, Greg, and I ran upstairs. We thought it would be better for her to get some of the anger out of her system. Greg wrestled with her until she was completely exhausted. The next day Judy visited her shrink, who prescribed a "rest." She was hospitalized soon after.

After Judy left for the hospital, Arthur felt more convinced that our "free school" atmosphere couldn't help some kids with their special problems. He remembered his words of assurance to Judy's father after she had run away and wondered whether the school had helped her at all.

Arthur had at first been hesitant about pushing for more structure in our community. His friendship with a clinical psychologist who had visited the school several times helped him overcome these fears. The psychologist had observed the dynamics of our community and felt that Arthur was playing the father role. He said that he was skeptical that any commune could survive unless it was organized like a family—with clearly defined father and mother figures. Arthur now felt comfortable about being the patriarch of our household. I thought it was foolish to reinforce the very roles that many kids were rebelling against. Why should we invest simple tasks like washing dishes with all the trauma of family quarrels?

Arthur and Ira tended to view the problems of our community from a psychoanalytical perspective. If relationships in the house were tense, they blamed personal "hangups." I felt that the conflicts between us had structural roots—that they could not be solved until we reorganized the project in a way that would make everybody feel comfortable. Our hassles would not disappear until we found a way to share leadership.

Psychiatry, I felt, dealt only with the symptoms of alienation, not its causes. Instead of encouraging the person to be himself, psychiatry sought to adjust people to "reality," to often intolerable conditions. Many of the kids had the same feeling. They had gone to guidance counselors, who blamed them, not the public school system, for their failures. They viewed shrinks as allies of their parents, as specialists in social adjustment.

Whenever Ira, Arthur, and I got together I felt they were using their psychoanalytic tools to dissect me. They wanted me to open up, but I felt too much like a patient on the couch to do that. We could never have a normal conversation. After I said something, they would often ask me; "What's your hangup?" or "Why did you use that word?" I was particularly bitter at one meeting when Ira exclaimed, after cross-examining me, that he couldn't trust me, because we weren't able to communicate.

Arthur began to talk about leaving the house and working part time at the school in the evenings. He explained the frustration he felt in a note he wrote to me.

> I wish you could see the condition of the dining room table upon which I'm writing this, the kitchen where I made my coffee (it smells like a sweet summer garbage dump), the living room and upstairs (the attic has been abandoned because of the overpowering smell of cat shit not cleaned up, abandoned). Or hear the constant noise. . . .
>
> I have other reasons though for doing what I plan. For one, I find very little willingness on any but a couple of students' parts to do the work necessary for learning what I have to teach. This may be my fault as a teacher, or the students' fault for not doing anything not immediately enjoyable . . . The point is I see no need for myself at the school during the day, the few students that really demonstrate a desire to learn with me I can easily work with in spare hours, and therefore no reason for me not to get a job. Related to this is the area of responsibility. Because I

am one of the four "officers" [he is talking about the officers of
our corporation], one of the two legally responsible people living
at the house, and because parents have placed a certain trust in
us, I feel I am responsible to a large degree for whatever happens
at the house. But I don't feel I can fulfill that responsibility,
there is no control over what they do at the house, or over who
comes in or even stays over. For instance, I just found out after
the fact, that there has been pot smoking. On that, because we
all did make a decision, I feel I can speak freely; but on other
things, because no consensus has been reached, I feel I can only
speak for myself, and that I won't do, that's a betrayal. If I am to
be held to blame, not only legally or morally by parents, but my
own conscience then I demand a certain degree of authority over
what goes on—how else can it be? All of these reasons compel me
to move. And my feelings of frustration, of being unable to do
anything when I see people not caring about each other, being
very content to see Alice cooking and shopping and meal planning every fucking day and not even offering any more than momentary help, when I see people refusing to face up to the reality
of our situation, who would rather go along feeling fine and
dandy and these are just little problems a little money will
work out, it bothers and bugs me, bothers the hell out of me,
frustrates and saddens me, takes away my smile and my sleep and
turns me into something I'd rather not be. Do you think we are
a success? I have seen many beautiful, exquisite things happen
at the school, seen people grow, seen people light up when love
was shown them, had people cry to me for the same reason, have
seen some lives change not imperceptibly at our school, and yet
I don't think we are a success. How many tears have you cried
over us? . . .

Because Randy Shaw and I lived several blocks away from
Park Road in a basement apartment, we were comfortably removed from the difficulties that Arthur had to face. We did not
constantly have to put our ideals to the test. When Bill Howe
asked if I would exchange places with him for a week, I refused. I was much less a total "anarchist" than Randy was. (I
put the word in quotes because it was bandied around in a way
that would have offended Bakunin and Kropotkin, who be-

lieved in structure if it was organic and responsive to the will of the members of the community.) I stood somewhere between the believers in total spontaneity and the advocates of a tight structure. We both, however, wanted a more loosely structured community than Arthur and Ira did.

Arthur decided to dramatize his dissatisfaction with the way things were going at Park Road by asking that his ideas be presented to all the members of the school for their approval. If his reforms of community policies were approved he would stay, and if they were turned down he would leave—at least this was how many of us interpreted Arthur's strategy. I remember that Greg said at the time that he wished Arthur had simply left Park Road when he had originally planned to. Now many people felt that he was giving us an ultimatum: either accept my views or else I'll leave the school.

Arthur had formed an alliance that included Ira, Steve, Bill, and himself. Because Ira had to work from nine till four, he was rarely able to be at the school. Most of his conceptions of the school he borrowed from Arthur, whom he trusted implicitly because of their long friendship. Bill (who had recently quit his job at Hamilton High School and was working full time in our project) was totally convinced of Arthur's sincerity and good intentions. He also found living at Park Road uncomfortable and chaotic.

Steve was the member of the group who was least committed to Arthur's ideas. But Arthur was the only person who spoke to Steve's feelings about the living conditions in the house. Steve was irritated that he couldn't sleep on any kind of stable schedule. He never had the peace and quiet to read the prepare for his classes. He thought that some kind of house organization would be better than the atmosphere of constant flux and disorder that pervaded our community.

From early in December until close to the end of the second week, activities at the school pretty much came to a halt. People who lived at the house and kids who lived with their families began to spend most of their time discussing the issues that divided our community. A sober, serious mood took over from the gaiety and élan that had once characterized our life at Park Road. I came into the house one day and saw a large group of people sitting around the dining room table. They were talking in serious tones about "the state of the school." It was like walking into a seminary.

Arthur's threat that he would leave the school if his proposals were not accepted made many people feel that our community was more fragile than it in fact was. The conflict that was developing forced people to choose sides. Factions began to form. Arthur and Ira tried to win converts; Greg and I organized a meeting at Randy Shaw's apartment to raise the morale of people who opposed Arthur's views. We excluded Arthur and Ira from the meeting because we felt that many of the kids would feel intimidated in their presence. To his credit, Randy was one of the few people who refused to become involved in the conflicts that were polarizing the community.

Things would not have been so tense if we had simply been debating concrete proposals for the organization of the school. In fact, neither side presented a real program. The struggle was more a battle between our egos, between different perceptions of self-interest. The people who opposed Arthur felt that his faction would crush their loose and relaxed life style if it won control of the school. Rumors were constantly floating around that Arthur and Ira wanted to expel anyone who was caught smoking dope in the house, that they wanted to institute a more academic routine in the school. Arthur and Ira, on the other hand, were appalled that the kids at Park Road were willing to live so "irresponsibly," with so little "love" for each other.

I had invested a lot of my own ego in the project; in part, I was trying to prove to myself that I was actually capable of organizing a free school. I wanted to prove that I could translate my ideas on experimental education into practice. Of all the older people I was the one most closely identified with the school, because I had done so much of the early organizing at Blair. When Arthur and Ira began to criticize the way the school was running, I took their remarks as a personal attack. I felt that they wanted to turn the school into one big "encounter group," a continuous therapy session. They wanted our community to turn in on itself; I wanted the school to be an instrument of radical social change. I remember saying that I would quit the project if Arthur and Ira got their way.

I was getting more tense; I wanted to get back to the classes that had been interrupted because of the crisis. I was angry with Arthur because, in my mind, he was primarily responsible for precipitating the conflicts that were absorbing all our energies. I was particularly irritated because he had given up trying to "teach."

At last he proposed we hold an all-school meeting to consider his criticisms and to propose reforms. But it was unclear whether the meeting would also vote on his proposals once and for all. Whatever happened, I was sure that the meeting would determine the fate of the project. My worst nightmare was that a victory for Arthur and Ira or a total stalemate would leave the school in a shambles.

Arthur invited his friend the clinical psychologist to come to the meeting, apparently to mediate the dispute. He reasoned that the psychologist could give us some very sound advice, because his interest in the outcome of the battle was much less subjective than ours. Right or wrong, I knew that the psychologist was firmly in Arthur's camp. And Arthur had asked very few people in the school if they wanted the psychologist to be present.

The fact that he had invited him to come without consulting the rest of us particularly incensed Greg and me. I spoke to Arthur and told him that I felt the psychologist would intimidate many of the kids, would discourage them from honestly expressing their feelings. I accused him of inviting an authority figure in order to manipulate the meeting. Greg tried to persuade Arthur not to have the psychologist. Since Arthur insisted on his presence, several of us—Randy, Greg, myself—decided to boycott the meeting. I wrote a broadside, which Randy signed and distributed to people just before the discussion began. It conveys the feelings I had at the time better than anything I can say here.

Experience teaches us that love does not consist in looking one another in the eye, rather in looking outward together in the same direction.   Antoine de Saint-Exupéry

I wanted to tell you why I'm not coming to the meeting tonight. The ugly atmosphere of the last few days has upset me deeply. At one point I thought we could sit down together and resolve our differences. I was willing to do this. The promoters of the meeting do not have this goal in mind. The way I understand it, it's all or nothing for them. Either accept our terms for staying in the school, or we'll leave. I have no desire to be given any more ultimatums or to be intimidated. Furthermore, when it was quite clear that Greg and I and a good number of other people thought it would be a bad thing for a psychiatrist to attend the meeting, our feelings were completely disregarded. Realizing this, it would be bad for me personally to attend. It would be hard not to be overwhelmed by the ugliness and rancor that is becoming so pervasive. I hope you will understand this feeling. If there is any truth to the statement that the school is "falling apart," it is not for the reasons suggested—inability to clean up dishes. . . . What was a wonderful social experiment—I should say still is—has resembled in the last two days a guilt-ridden seminary. I intend to continue working with the school and doing the best I can do to see it and its example continue.

Peace,
Joel

The meeting took place, but because such an important segment of the community had opposed the way it had been set up, Arthur and Ira decided to arrange another one. Kathy, a student, and Dave left the meeting because they couldn't take the "shouting." Many of the people who remained didn't live at the house. Since the majority of people there agreed to his proposals for more structure in the house, Arthur felt the meeting had gone very well.

I remember the evening of the second meeting very well. Almost everyone in the school was there except Randy. (I had tried to encourage a number of kids who hadn't been at the first meeting to come, so that their voices could be heard.) The usual large crowd had eaten dinner and polished off a large amount of wine. People were sitting in the living room, the dining room, on the staircase, waiting for the fireworks to begin.

Greg and I decided that we should do something to counter-act the somber mood that usually characterized our meetings. We quickly worked out a strategy. We would both get dressed up, smoke cigars, and carry several six-packs of Colt 45 Malt Liquor. Maybe after watching our exhibition, people would take themselves a little less seriously.

The meeting started about eight o'clock, very soon after Greg and I had arrived and plopped our six-packs down on the dining room table. The meeting lasted only thirty minutes be-fore it turned into a "love feast." Very early in the discussion I made a statement—which I don't even remember—that Ira objected to. He said it was incomprehensible. A confrontation between Bill Howe and Audrey followed. The dialogue be-tween them went something like this:

Andrey: I don't always understand everything that Joel says, but I love him anyway. I'd really like to kiss and hug him.

Bill Howe: Don't you feel the same way about Arthur and Ira?

Audrey: No.

Bill: Maybe that's because they made you and Charlie feel guilty that you weren't contributing money to the house.

On that note Audrey broke down and started sobbing. Char-lie, Greg, and I got up from the table to comfort her. We all hugged and embraced each other. The meeting was, for all practical purposes, over. It was fated to break up; all we needed was a pretext. The seeds of division had been sown long ago. Soon most of the other people at the meeting left the table and joined us. We embraced and hugged each other; we laughed and we cried. Perhaps this was the only way we could respond to the impersonality of meetings—the only way we could affirm the sense of unity we felt.

Arthur and Ira stayed far removed from the circle. Greg went over to Arthur to ask him to join us, but he refused. Greg began to sob. Arthur had once been a close friend of his, a person in whom he had frequently confided. Arthur, Ira, Bill, and Alice left the school for good that evening. Steve was still undecided about what he would do. But in a few days he had definitely committed himself to stay with us.

Greg, Steve, Dave, and I drove off a few days later to Yellow Springs, Ohio, to visit Antioch College. After the split we just wanted to get away and unwind. I was still really shell-shocked. I was still not ready to face the fact that our community had fragmented and that we were now at a new stage of development. We all vowed not to talk about the hassles of the past weeks, but they kept coming up no matter how much we tried to repress them.

We spent a relaxing four days in Yellow Springs, where we stayed with my brother, who is a student at the college. One memorable evening we realized how much tension we had stored up over the past month. The four of us went to a Greek lamb roast at the outdoor education center. An Antioch student had organized the affair as a senior honors project; it would be a Greek bacchanal complete with eating, drinking, folk dancing. We all got very drunk on the huge quantities of Greek wine that were served up to the crowd. I will always remember the sight of Greg and Dave romping through the center, merrily drunk, holding huge lamb bones, climbing on the rafters.

4. Movement and Learning

Many of the older people in the school, myself included, were anxious about the fact that people were constantly joining and then leaving, that it was impossible to establish any sort of stable program. But transience was also the source of some of our most intense learning experiences.

Many of the kids wanted to travel, to hitchhike, to experience the simple liberty that adults take for granted but that the state denies to young people—freedom of movement. I remember an evening in early September shortly after Jeremiah had returned from several months of hitchhiking and riding boxcars across the continent. On an impulse, Jeremiah and

Charlie decided to take off and hitchhike to Harpers Ferry, where they planned to camp out. I was annoyed that they were both leaving at a time when we were organizing our program for the fall. In my opinion they were being irresponsible, they were copping out. But I repressed these feelings and never expressed them to Jeremiah or Charlie.

Later in the year Jeremiah and his friend Larry were planning to go north to New England. Arthur drove them to the train yards, where they planned to hop a freight. He was disturbed that Jeremiah and Larry were traveling all of the time rather than being with the community.

"How come you want to leave again?" Arthur asked.

"No reason," said Larry. "We just feel like moving. I think best at sixty mph."

"Yeah," Arthur said, "but what about your responsibility to our community?"

"Arthur," Jeremiah answered, "we just have a different idea of community. Our community is an open one, it includes everyone. It's out there. If you restrict yourself to a narrow community, then you stop learning. The experience no longer 'furthers.' "

Jeremiah was the most avid traveler in our community. He felt that people should feel free to leave the school at any time and not feel guilty about it. The times he returned from his many trips that year were among our most wonderful moments. He would come back from New England, the West Coast, the Shenandoahs, the Appalachian Trail, and Harpers Ferry and regale us with stories, anecdotes, and tales of the road.

Jeremiah, a tall, lanky guy, went on his travels carrying no extra clothing and only a few coins in the pants he wore. A vegetarian, he cooked lentils and other simple foods for himself. He attached great spiritual significance to his journeys and frequently took with him the *I Ching* and Gibran. Jeremiah had moved a great distance from the time I first met him at Montgomery Blair, where he was a political activist, a real fighter for student power. His first trip across the country on his own turned his head around.

Jeremiah made quite an impact on Sam, the youngest student in the school, age twelve. One week in early October, Jeremiah and Larry, his traveling companion, who had dropped out from the University of Buffalo, took him along on a camping trip they were making to the Shenandoahs. They all hiked, and Jeremiah and Larry fasted. Sam also tried fasting but was not able to keep it up. Sam describes the trip as one of the peak learning experiences he had that year—it involved real risks.

People were continually getting involved in the project who had important experiences and skills to share with us. Randy took a trip up to the CNVA (Committee for Non-Violent Action) farm in Connecticut and returned with an old friend of his, Henry, who was a talented artist. Henry brought with him his portfolio of paintings, etchings, and drawings. At about the same time Marion, a friend of a friend of Steve's, arrived from Boston. She also was an artist. Together and quite spontaneously they stirred up an interest in art. The dining room table became a workbench. As Henry put it, "I would be sitting at the kitchen table drinking coffee and someone would burst in and say 'Look what I've just done.'" Kathy used paints, Dave used pen and ink, Steve rediscovered pastels. A few people did copper enameling. Henry's portraits of people in the school hung on the walls. In a setting like this, where art was fully integrated into the daily life of the commune, formal classes were largely irrelevant.

Brooke Higdon and Judy Reichsman, two co-op students, arrived from Antioch to spend three months with us in January. Judy moved into the house, and Brooke stayed with his parents. Their dance class took up where the nonverbal group left off. They had very specific body exercises to loosen the muscles. At the same time people in the class used the newly understood body language to convey feelings. The class met three times a week and usually five people were involved. Kathy thought it was the best class we had all year.

Marc Sommer, a young writer, organized a creative writing course during the fall. Ed De Grazia, a lawyer who specialized in taking censorship cases (*I Am Curious* (*Yellow*), *Naked Lunch*), visited us one evening and decided to initiate a study group in mythology. Simon, a former student at Blair, and Sam had already organized a class to investigate Indian culture. Pippa, an English girl who was visiting Washington, heard about the school, came, and started teaching basic nutrition and cooking. Felix, a local freak, invited himself into the house and began to interest people in drawing cartoons and making film strips of them.

Greg had taken classes in arc welding at Bell Vocational School and was now ready to apply his skills to the making of metal sculpture. Greg was working closely with Karl Hess, a disaffected speech writer for Barry Goldwater, who now felt that the best hope for the libertarian Right lay in an alliance with the Left. He gave Greg the key to his studio and encouraged him to use it and his tools whenever he wanted.

Simon moved into the school during the Christmas holidays after dropping out of music school in Baltimore. As his friend, Norm Solomon, put it: "[Simon] passed up Brandeis and a prosperous future as a skilled physicist, and left home; he's been busted for drugs, spent eight days in a Baltimore jail with queers and bad-doin' guards for not paying a traffic fine; he's been hassled by cops dozens of times for doing things like walking through the streets barefoot at 2:00 A.M. or playing his flute in deserted school buildings."

Simon was always doing music. In January, at the Counter-Inaugural demonstration, Simon led the band of Yippies. Charlie started going to a local Buddhist temple and began a regimen of daily chanting. Jeremiah and Larry continued to hitchhike and ride freight trains, always returning to visit us at the end of their trips. Charlie once called the school a "crucible," into which poured countless different people with unique experiences and ideas.

Our transience made living in the commune difficult. We were always having guests—during the Counter-Inaugural there were dozens. Sometimes they stayed a week—sometimes months. Steve remembers the time Mad John came to visit:

> The first time I met "Mad John" he was walking around our Park Road house wearing only a towel. Jeremiah had met him

and invited him to stay at our house. Mad John had an almost supernatural countenance which commanded awe everywhere he went. His eyelids drooped mysteriously. He didn't walk—he seemed to float on some sort of aura. He spent his time drawing detailed portraits of people in the house, interspersing them with drawings of a Hindu-type female with a calm expression and sensuous lips.

Whenever he was around, people stopped whatever they were doing. In the middle of one of our circuitous, trivial meetings he interrupted us talking of poetry, of some other reality. Many of us, absorbed in our smaller worlds, became overly fearful and defensive about his presence. I thought of him as a charlatan who used "mysticism" to gain control, a sleepy-eyed Rasputin. Yet he was kind, gentle, and helpful around the house. He sensed that his presence was disturbing the house. As soon as we hinted that we were crowded, he left the house.

Not everyone was as sensitive and cooperative as Mad John. I don't know how he found us, but Herbie just started coming over. The first night he told us how depressed he was and hinted that he was suicidal. Some people drove him home and went back to check later to make sure he hadn't done away with himself. He was broke and his girl friend was pregnant and never wanted to see him again. He began borrowing from us—five dollars here, a dollar there. He lost his apartment and needed a place to stay. So the Park Road commune let him move in "temporarily," since it was hard to refuse anyone so supplicatory and pathetic.

When we received our phone bill we discovered he had run up a seventy-dollar bill—he had been calling his girl friend out of town quite frequently. When we told him he couldn't stay any more he would sneak in at night to make his calls. Finally he stopped coming by. "If I ever see that bastard again, I'll kill him," said Greg, still bitter a year later.

Steve felt the same way about Felix:

Felix had come originally to teach cartooning and photography, but now he only used the place to eat and sleep. At mealtimes, he would crawl out of nowhere and eat more and faster than anyone else. Once, during a meeting, he exploded a firecracker. This was too much for me. "The next time you intend to do that," I suggested, "stick it up your ass before you light the fuse." A while later, Dave told me how annoyed he was when Felix set off the firecracker. "So I walked outside to cool off," he said. I was so glad to see Felix go, that I gave him my knapsack.

Kids came and went at a remarkable rate. Kathy Becker recalls:

> I had a hard time figuring out who was in the school. Sometimes people would come by and zap!—they were in the school. When Cookie first came with her parents, I think I was the only one there. They all came in and sat down and I said, "Oh, hello," and Cookie said, "Oh, yes, I'm coming here." It was really weird. How could she be sure she wanted to go if she'd never been here before? And I'd never heard of or seen her before.

Steve also felt uncomfortable when he first met Cookie:

> She looked like the stereotyped motorcycle chick—short, bleached-blond hair, tight pants and boots. Her parents were overly polite—they were eager to drop her off. She had been a runaway, involved with sex and hard drugs. She was very self-destructive. Our school was a last resort. "We've tried everything," her parents seemed to say, "we don't want anything more to do with her. She's become one of your kind. Now *you* handle her."
>
> Late in January her parents dropped her off for good. They called her Charlotte, but she insisted we call her Cookie. The first night she stayed with us, we all played an impromptu charade in the living room. We took an object—like a scarf or umbrella—and thought up as many scenes as we could using these "props." We had a lot of fun and she seemed to relax.
>
> The next day, Greg told me he found some "works" (needles used for heroin) in her possession. "I told her I never wanted to see them again and I threw them into the woods. I don't think she'll ever find them."

We began receiving long-distance calls from a lawyer in Texas who wanted his son to go to the school.

"Well," Steve said reluctantly, "let me try to explain the school . . ."

"That's okay. I'm flying down to bring him in."

The next Sunday he came with his son and a journalist friend from D.C. "I came to drop off the boy. This is Ralph."

They sat down for a quick cup of coffee. The father put three hundred-dollar bills on the table.

"Are you sure you want him to go here?" Steve asked.

"He'll like it."

"Uh—would you like to see some literature on the school?"

He hesitated. "Nope," he answered. As he left he said; "Now I trust that the boy will be president of his class by nightfall."

In spite of, or because of, the flux, the kids living at Park Road began to develop a very tightly knit community. They were always doing things together. At least once a week Randy would drive a group of eight to ten kids somewhere—usually to Gifford's (an ice-cream parlor in Silver Spring, Maryland) or to Hofberg's (the only really Jewish delicatessen the Washington area could boast). Randy took great joy in trying to freak out the clientele at these suburban enclaves. He once made a production of picking imaginary bugs from his thick beard and loudly stomping on them.

Music was also a unifying experience. The loud music of Hendrix, Cream, and Joplin complemented our frenetic existence. Every Sunday for several months people from the school went to the "grok," a rock concert held at American University. The élan the commune group felt really came out when we went to one of these events. One of the most memorable experiences of the year occurred when Steve went with Kathy's mother and a group from the school to hear the Cream play in Baltimore. Steve describes it. "The concert took place in the local basketball palace, a terrible place for music. Unmindful of the stifling atmosphere, our group began to bang on the seats and dance in the aisles. We took home a strange musical energy as a bond between us. All the way home in the car we sang and drummed and waved to people."

We also made our own music. Simon brought music to Park Road. He was an accomplished flute player, had recently learned the blues harp, and now was picking up the guitar. He owned a conga drum, which Steve began to play. A friend from Baltimore sometimes brought his drum set over. A few times Pat and Dan, two students who lived at home, brought their electric guitars. Even before we had the dance class, people seldom related to music in a passive way. I remember walking into Park Road and seeing people dancing to "In-A-Gadda-Da-Vida," by the Iron Butterfly.

Taking drugs together was the group experience that, more than anything else, made the Park Road commune a cohesive one. Kids usually smoked grass and hash or dropped acid elsewhere (usually in Rock Creek Park) and then came to the house. (Occasionally they would break the rules and do drugs in the commune.) The older people living at Park Road were annoyed when they took acid and stayed up all night. One night Steve got very angry when a large group started tripping around midnight, began playing rock music, crowded into closets, and kept up a constant uproar until four in the morning.

Tripping also brought people closer together; it was a time for embracing, for expressions of real tenderness. Sam talks about the time a group was tripping. They all went upstairs to the "community room" (a bedroom on the second floor that was strewn with mattresses) and began kissing and hugging each other. People, he said, would frequently concentrate their energies on comforting a person who had gotten frightened because of his experience on drugs. Sam felt that people living in the commune often expressed the same spirit when they weren't on drugs. If someone was on a "bummer," or felt unhappy, other people in the house would try to soothe him.

I was always a bit uneasy about kids in the school taking acid, even though I enjoyed smoking grass and hash. But I felt paranoid about smoking with them. The few times I did were very mellow experiences. Once a group of us smoked some hash at Randy's apartment and got really wrecked. Sam started reciting Etruscan folk tales, I read verses from Baudelaire's *Les Fleurs du Mal*. We went back to Park Road and began playing the Beatles' and Stones' albums in chronological order.

Drugs confronted us with real legal problems. What if we were busted? What if a kid freaked out while he was under our "supervision"? Steve returned from a trip to find the people had been using drugs in the house while he had been gone. He confronted Margaret and Sam, allegedly the ones who had brought in the drugs.

"If this place gets busted, I go to jail, not you. I'm over twenty-one. I signed the lease. That's why I don't want dope here," he said. "I'm saying this not as an authority but as someone whom you're living with and ought to protect."

But drugs in the school had more serious implications than this. Could we cope with a bad trip? One night Steve found Sam tripping in the house.

> I was annoyed, since we recently decided that there would be no more tripping at our house. I became more upset when Sam became sick. He had to be carried to the bathroom to throw up. Afterward he lay down in one of the bedrooms, curled up like a fetus, babbling and drooling. I freaked out—I'd never seen anyone deteriorate like this. "It's horrible—I'm dying," he moaned over and over. We sat there for an hour trying to comfort him, holding his hand, but he remained just the same. Someone called the free clinic, but they could offer little help. Everyone seemed more optimistic than I was. "I've seen this before," Henry said. "He'll pull out of it."
>
> I was ready to take him to the hospital. I realized I had to call his parents first, since he was under age. His parents' line was busy. I was happy for the slight reprieve. Again I went up to sit with him. Now he seemed improved—he no longer was drooling and his speech was more articulate. During the next two hours he improved, so I went to bed.
>
> I went downstairs the next morning to find Sam sitting on the dining room table calmly playing his guitar. The entire dining room and kitchen had been cleaned. "Jesus, Sam, you really had us worried. You had a bad time last night."
>
> "What do you mean 'bad time'? It was the best trip I've ever had. It was fantastic!"

Even though strong bonds tied us to each other, communal problems persisted. Alice had been running the kitchen through December. Now few people wanted to cook, and food buying was sporadic and capricious. Once Randy and a few others returned from a discount food store in Baltimore with a case of vinegar and a case of hamburger relish. Steve hit the ceiling. "We can't even afford hamburgers!" he shouted. The shopping crew answered that if he didn't like what they had bought he could do it himself.

We once counted twenty-four people at the dinner table. Besides the eleven people living at Park Road, seven of us came from Randy's house a few blocks away. Others would just be "around" at dinner time. Our group would generally arrive a half hour before dinner. "Well, what do we have tonight?" Randy would ask. When we sat down to eat Randy would scream in jest, "God, what sort of shit is THIS? It isn't edible, is it?"

Meals were louder than ever, quips going back and forth, people eating quickly. Once Steve spent a few hours preparing a meal and was called to the phone. When he returned there was nothing left. "Vultures! Hyenas!" he screamed. As he settled into his more customary sarcasm he remarked that there were two kinds of people at the house—the quick and the hungry.

As the food situation deteriorated, people began to hoard cookies, crackers, and other shit food in their rooms. Others would make lightning raids into the kitchen in search of a quick snack, leaving it in a shambles. Steve began eating in restaurants more frequently. Henry, Barbara, and Judy Reichsman, in obvious reaction to the loud, frenetic pace of dinner, became macrobiotics. They ate separately from the rest of us, quietly and slowly.

5. *We Relate to the Greater Community*

Much of our activity the first year centered around the commune. This sometimes confused and disturbed kids who lived at home and commuted to the school. During the commune crisis in December all activities virtually stopped. At other times kids would come to Park Road or Friends' Meeting House for classes to find that some communal activity (cleaning or food buying) had prevented them from happening.

One morning Bill and Arthur went to the lumberyard to pick up boards and cinder blocks to make bookshelves. They returned just as Steve was to begin a nonverbal class.

"Let's get everyone to pitch in and get these books up. They've been lying around the living room for a month," Arthur said.

"Well, I planned to have a class now," Steve said.

"We went through all of this trouble to get these things. This is a good communal project for everyone to get involved with. Maybe your class can wait," Bill and Arthur suggested.

Steve did postpone his class, but many of the noncommune kids involved felt that the class was more important than a building project. Our relationships in the house, our communal problems, often informed the discussions we had in class. At their best the classes were a medium through which we could share our varied personal experiences.

Once in a philosophy class a group of us were discussing André Gide's *The Immoralist,* the story of a classical scholar who abandoned his bourgeois existence for a life of travel and sensuality. The novel struck a responsive chord in all of us— the eight of us sitting on chairs and on the floor in Randy Shaw's apartment. Jeremiah started talking about himself, about wanting to live a quiet, mystical life—traveling was a spiritual experience for him. He was tired of words, of long analytical raps. Words just obscured personal feelings, he said.

I said that I could not liberate myself, except as part of a social movement that would free all people from bondage. Jeremiah's life style and my own sharply clashed. We had once worked closely to change conditions at Montgomery Blair. But Jeremiah now had abandoned politics. Dave, less sure of his own philosophy, was puzzled by what both of us had said. He asked us both questions.

Gide's novel had helped us to open up, to reveal ourselves and our visions, our hesitancies, our doubts. We exhausted ourselves—it was so intense. Kathy, Dave, and a few others wanted to unwind, and they left to take a walk. It was a magical, luminous morning. My doubts, my discomfort about being a teacher, dissolved in the spontaneity of it all.

Throughout the year we invited speakers to our house to discuss the political action they were involved in. I hoped this would illuminate the same questions and conflicts we had been dealing with in our classes. In the fall we asked two people to come to talk about their trips to Cuba—Sue Orrin, a Women's Liberation activist, and Blase Bompane, one of the Maryknoll priests who had worked in Guatemala. Randy prepared a fantastic Mexican meal, which all fifteen or twenty of us sat down to eat.

After dinner Sue and Blase talked about their impressions of Cuba. Both gave lyrical accounts of the solidarity of the Cuban people, of the zest with which the peasants were building a socialist nation. Blase said that Cuba was the only country in Latin America he had been to where he had not seen people starving in the streets. Their talk hit home when they described how the revolution was creating new kinds of men and women—people who wanted to live and work cooperatively. Sue talked about a new ethic developing in the country, about the pressure on each citizen, whether intellectual or laborer, to work in the cane fields.

The students in our school were fiercely individualistic—they wanted to do their own thing. Dave argued that the Cuban system, like any revolutionary alternative, would turn out to be just as coercive as our society. Larry Aaronson, Sue, and I tried to explain how competitive individualism in a Third World country kept people down and reinforced exploitation. We said that people in Cuba had a different concept of freedom, of what it meant to be a person—that an individual can only fulfill himself as part of a community—than Western societies have.

Blase explained that his attitude toward violence had changed as a result of his work in Latin America. Revolutionary violence, he felt, was a better alternative for most people than submission to the "official" violence—the poverty, disease, and exploitation—of an oligarchical system. As a result of the evening's discussion Randy, Greg, Dave, and I went to a conference on revolution in Latin America sponsored by the Committee for Non-Violent Action at their farm in Voluntown, Connecticut.

Later in the year we invited Al McSurely, an organizer in Appalachia, to speak about his experiences. At about the same time the Melvilles, who had participated in the burning of draft files in Maryland, spent an evening with us. Randy and I had gone to Baltimore with several students earlier in the year to attend the trial of the Catonsville Nine (a group that included the Melvilles). Since there was no room in the courtroom, we joined in the picketing outside the federal building.

During the Counter-Inaugural ceremonies in January, or the "In-hog-uration," as the Yippies called it, we threw our house open to friends, friends of friends, and freaks from all over. A few liked our house so much that they delayed leaving for a week. The sponsors set up a large tent near the Washington monument which would house the day's speakers and the evening's In-hog-ural Ball. Randy and I were running a morning workshop on alternative schools in a church in southwest Washington.

Steve was at the tent before the afternoon march began and attended the evening's festivities:

> For the first time, we noted three distinct factions of the movement all confronting each other. One was the veterans of Chicago, the nascent Weathermen, bent on street action and confrontation with the police. Another faction was the movement "establishment," the people who had been giving speeches for the last five years. They droned on with predictable rhetoric, talking to the same people over and over again. All of a sudden a band of colorfully dressed Yippies led by Simon playing his flute made its way through the tent chanting "Shut the fuck up! Shut the fuck up!" while banging drums and cymbals. Outside Yippie cheerleaders shouted for heroes "Jer-ry Ru-bin," "Col-onel Sanders," and "George Me-tesky."
>
> That night ⅔ of the school drove to the In-hog-ural Ball. De-

spite the mud, the crowd, and the chaos, we danced wildly in a circle and threw beach balls across the tent, hyperventilated and passed joints.

On Inauguration Monday the more serious militants demonstrated. Simon and Cookie were picked up by the police and accused of throwing rocks. Both were innocent. The cops jumped Cookie first, thinking she was a guy. When Simon rushed to defend her, they got him instead. People at Park Road spent the night talking with Simon's parents, calling lawyers, calling the jail. They finally found out where he was, and Randy picked him up.

Later in the year we tried to relate to other projects like our own. In January, Fred Newman spoke to us about Centers for Change, an alternative university commune in New York City, organized very much like our project. A few weeks later Randy and Steve took a group of people up to New York to spend a few days with the Centers people. In the spring Mrs. Becker, Kathy's mother, took Kathy and another girl to visit Centers. In May, John Holt and Edgar Friedenberg came to speak. Holt came soon before we moved from Park Road, and I remember him rolling up his sleeves to help us remove some graffiti from our walls.

We understimated how important it was to get some perspective on our work. Kathy recalls:

> In March Joel, myself and a few other people attended an "alternatives" conference in Woodstock, New York. Up until then we had been really introspective, not really connected with people outside. Now at the conference, I talked with some people from Philadelphia and everything, all my feelings about the school, came out. I said that people were unwilling to relate to each other, we were going through meaningless action, we were goalless. We didn't know what we were doing or why. I told them everything and the most amazing thing happened. They said, "Yeah, it's happened to us too—it's happened to everyone here." It felt good to know that it wasn't just us, that we weren't bad or incompetent.

Initially we were suspicious of parents, especially after Judy's father tried to remove her from the school. But as the year progressed some of the kids' parents became quite close to us. Mrs. Becker was always coming by to see how we were doing and was always willing to help out. A number of times she brought over large bags of groceries. She also taught French and Spanish at the school. People would go over to Norm Solomon's or Jeremiah's house for dinner or would eat Sunday breakfast at Sam's house in College Park. As their children began to get excited about learning again, the initial skepticism that many of the parents had about the school left them. Now that they were doing something they really wanted to do, the kids were less inclined to rebel against their parents, to make them scapegoats.

In April we had a parents' meeting, the first in months. Kathy's father said, "I think the school has been good therapy for Kathy, but I don't think she's getting a good education." He related an incident that showed she didn't realize that two historical figures were contemporaries, "That's totally irrelevant," Greg's father said. "I'm a scientist, and I think I'm pretty well informed. I don't know that bit of information, nor do I care to know about it. The most significant educational experience for Kathy has been living at the house!"

Our school, of course, attracted the attention of the media. A reporter from the *Evening Star* asked how we would feel about his doing a feature story on the school. I felt an article would help to communicate our ideas about experimental education. It might even encourage some readers to start their own schools. Most everyone supported me. However, there were some people, like Sam, who felt that our increased visibility would bring the police and other authorities to our doorstep.

The reporter spent a good deal of time at the school, talked with a lot of people, and wrote a pretty fair piece about us. It became the lead story of the *Star's Sunday Magazine* (February 23, 1969). But he often communicated what he had learned about the school in a standard journalistic framework. He focused on the personalities of the older people much more than we would have liked. He described my "rabbinical-style" beard and Steve's "vaguely Cuban-revolutionist longish black hair and beard." He referred to me as the "guiding guru" of the school.

By portraying us as "super stars," the reporter obscured the strong participation of the kids in shaping the character of the school. The article had the effect of reinforcing an authority position I was very uncomfortable with. There were other things about the way the piece was presented that I didn't like. The cover photo, a flamboyant shot of some of the freaky members of the school, played up the bizarreness of the project rather than its actual content or program. We of course allowed ourselves to be exploited in this way. Another picture showed a group of kids lounging in a bedroom strewn with mattresses. To a respectable reader it probably looked like an opium den. The reporter also mentioned the address of the Park Road commune; obviously we should have insisted that he omit it. Now anyone who wanted to harass us would know where we were.

It is too easy to blame the reporter for doing an article we didn't like. In our own innocence we brought this fate upon ourselves. We did not have a sufficient grasp of how the media operate, particularly of how they treat movement groups. The media have a marvelous way of legitimizing them—by elevating colorful personalities to media heroes. They portray the project or organization as a form of theater designed to titillate a mass audience. The worst effect of all of this is that radicals themselves sometimes begin to take the media images seriously. Then they begin to act like celebrities; life begins to imitate art. (We did not fully learn our lesson. Later we permitted a film crew from one of the local TV stations to do a program on us for Martin Agronsky's show.)

Sam was right. The article did tip off the authorities, and they soon began harassing us. One morning, a little bit drowsy, I answered the phone and a woman at the other end of the line asked, "Is this Mr. Denker?" She was the census supervisor for the Department of Pupil Personnel of the D.C. public schools. She asked if the *Sunday Star* article had quoted me correctly as saying, "In Washington anyone can start a school, there's no accrediting requirement." I hedged a little but eventually said yes. She was very anxious to assert her bureaucratic prerogatives, to inform me that her department had authority over all schools in the District. She seemed concerned about the condition of our "children"; she wondered if we would mind if someone from her department sat in on some of our classes.

But her classic question went something like this: "I don't quite know how to ask you this—but do you have a mental hygienist for your children?" I: "You mean a psychiatrist?" She: "Yes." I decided that I should try to buy some time, since I didn't want to issue a blanket invitation to her department. I asked her to send me all the forms that we were supposed to fill out. This was the beginning of my relationship with this school official, whom I never met but to whom I sent a number of long, bureaucratic letters.

A week after the article appeared we received a visit from the representatives of the D.C. Housing Department. We later learned that they had a file of letters complaining about our presence in the neighborhood. When they arrived they insisted that this was just a routine inspection. They told us that there were more people living in the house than the law permitted, that we could not use the attic for sleeping, and that we should correct these violations as soon as possible. Our landlord had never told us about these regulations when he permitted us to have eleven people living in the house.

The housing division overlooked the worst excesses of slum landlords but was perfectly willing to harass a group of powerless people living in a commune. Officials from the department continued to pester us throughout the spring. Later we were told that we would have to vacate the house unless we applied for a rooming-house permit, for which you had to pay a large fee.

After it became clear that we would have to move, we decided as a group to leave the city. We realized the contradiction of our living in a black area—we could leave, they couldn't. Our kids would walk down Mount Pleasant Street, unwittingly conspicuous with blond hair and hippie garb. To local black kids we were the "hippies in the corner house."

They resented us and a few times tried to hustle us. Steve was very upset the time this happened to Greg and Dave:

One evening someone brought over some wine, and Greg and Dave became very drunk. A little while later some local black youths, who had come by once before out of curiosity, paid us a return visit. Having grown up in a poor section of Brooklyn, I knew what it felt like to be hustled, and I was reluctant to go through the experience again. I chided myself for my paranoia but, nevertheless, tried to keep an eye on the kids. Greg and Dave, though, were both eager to talk with the visitors and let them come upstairs.

After they left we discovered some wristwatches and money were missing. Greg and Dave were especially upset because they wanted very much to establish some sort of rapport with the blacks. Greg said that one of the kids was his friend. My bitterness came out: "Don't you know that those kids were only up here to steal? Any sign of friendship was purely accidental."

Greg: "Well, I don't care about my property. Besides, what reason do they have to trust US?"

Steve: "I don't understand you! Why should you feel guilty for being a victim? I'm sure those guys don't feel guilty."

Dave: "I really want to be friends with these people. I thought we were having a good rap. But I'd rather risk losing some stuff than close off any opportunity to talk with them."

Greg became more upset as the conversation continued in this manner. I realized that I was telling them not to trust people. Even if my judgment had been right, was I justified in laying my paranoia on others? I was upset and confused myself and decided to leave. I ran over to Randy Shaw's place and tried to explain everything to Joel, who was sick in bed. Soon Greg and Dave were on the phone, very apologetic and very drunk: "We're sorry, Steve. We love you. We're coming over to pick you up."

I couldn't understand what they were apologizing for. In a few minutes they staggered over, and both hugged me. "We love you, Steve!"

Then they walked over to Joel, who was extremely confused by the whole scene. "We love you too, Joel," they said and began to hug him.

"Uh, I have a cold," Joel replied, trying to move away.

Greg and Dave were both sitting now. I realized that they

would have a hard time moving if we stayed any longer, so I suggested that they leave. "Come on, Kathy," said Greg, and I noticed he was talking to the radiator. I walked the two blocks home, dragging both of them, who had come to take me home. When we got to the house all of us started to hug each other. I felt myself engulfed. Greg and I could not resolve our differences. Yet neither of us could bear the tension either. We all hugged in recognition of this.

6. *Families Are for Leaving*

Steve recalls:

In the wake of worsening house disorder, I became unbearable. I got angry, petty, at times crazy. I tyrannized the house. I considered leaving for a while. Perhaps if I left, the kids at the house could solve their problems more easily.

Dave also had the urge to leave at that time—spending February in Washington is always a disturbing prospect. We decided to go to California "before it fell into the ocean." Within a few days I had gotten a driveaway car to Seattle and we were on our way west.

Traveling cleared our heads. I felt free from the audio and visual noise of our commune, free from the responsibility of "running" the school. We were free to look and be fascinated by things—the plains, the Rockies, the redwoods. I wished that everyone could be on the trip—in separate vehicles, though. We found California lush and green in the middle of February. She was a magical mistress who gave us rides and joints and smiles, asking nothing in return. I knew the pleasure of being a guest rather than a host.

One afternoon Dave and I and some friends climbed the Berkeley hills and sat looking out at the ocean. Some people came by and gave us wine. Later they played music for us. I picked up a blues harp and played along. The guitar player told me to keep the harp if I wanted to. In contrast to our commune, meals here had a silent, slow, religious feeling. A few of us would begin cooking unrelated dishes separately. Magically, everything would be ready at the same time, and all the separate dishes blended together. These meals seemed to last for hours.

I took acid for the first time, too much acid, and it was scary. When I came down I felt drained and cleansed, a little less edgy, more mellow. After two weeks in Berkeley, Dave and I both decided to return to Washington. We had left no California address, so we had no way of knowing what was going on at the school. We discovered that we were eager to get back; we made the return trip in four days.

Steve left because of the disorder. While he was gone the people in Randy's house began to cook and eat separately, taking some pressure off Park Road. Later, in the spring, the kids at Park Road, without help or encouragement from Steve, decided to set up a cooking and cleaning schedule, which they pretty much adhered to. Yet individually we were restless. We had spent the winter together and were ready to move on. After Dave and Steve returned from California they stirred up excitement with their tales of the West Coast.

Randy and a few others left for California around the first of April. Two weeks later Randy called us from Berkeley. "It's really great out here," he said. "I want to stay another month, maybe forever."

At first Steve felt hurt, upset, that Randy was "deserting" us. But Randy obviously had chosen what was best for him and was circuitously asking our approval. Steve told him he'd prefer him to stay with us, but it was his decision to make. "And don't feel guilty about it," Steve added.

Dave, Roger, and Greg began planning to leave for California around the first of May and could talk of little else. For nearly a month the rest of us were obliged to hear how lucky they were to be leaving for the holy land and how Washington was such a useless and decadent scene. Not much consolation for those of us who remained. Finally they left, and although we loved them, we felt a great relief.

CHAPTER IV

Steve: The Second Year

1. *Starting Again*

After Greg, Dave, and the others had left we set out to rebuild the school. When we started a year before, we had been excited and adventuresome, eager to leave the sterile, placid school system. Now we were somewhat subdued, drained by the intensity and insecurity of the past year. Those who remained sought a more stable, more comfortable existence. Henry and Barbara were expecting a baby and hoped to find a more comfortable place where Henry could concentrate on his art. Simon had been through a lot in the past year. He had been busted, left school in Baltimore, and then moved in with us. For the past three months he had been involved in a deep but turbulent relationship with Cookie. They, too, needed some breathing space.

Joel and I also wanted a more stable living situation. At the same time we hoped to open the school up to more people—to bring it out of its self-centered hibernation. We pushed for a move to the suburbs, so that we could have greater impact on white middle-class kids and their parents. We wanted to create a school structure independent of the ups and downs of the commune. If we expanded to two or three communes, no one place would be the center of the school. We felt that the communes engaged in parallel struggles would give us the perspective we had lacked the first year.

Henry and Simon did not wholeheartedly share our vision of a more tightly organized project. But we worked together finding a new house and attracting students for the fall with an eagerness reminiscent of our early days at Madison Street. Henry and Barbara quickly found us a house in Takoma Park, a small town outside Washington. Joel, Kathy, Monte—a student who had joined us a month earlier—and I wrote a new leaflet, which we began to distribute early in June. During May we held frequent organizational meetings to report our progress. During the past months meetings had been tense, guilt-ridden sessions where people defended whatever they were doing or not doing for the school. I was astounded to see how smoothly these spring meetings went, how well we shared the work.

Even during this period of renewed energy our differences cropped up. When we moved to Jefferson Avenue in Takoma Park in June, Simon and Cookie moved into a part of the house that had once been an "efficiency apartment" and had a separate entrance. They had their own kitchen and insisted on eating separately. Joel and I were slightly annoyed when Simon spray-painted a huge red peace symbol on the door to broadcast our arrival. We had hoped to relate to this community differently from Mount Pleasant—now once again we would be stereotyped as hippies.

Late in June the Stern Foundation notified us that we had received a $10,000 grant. Despite our joy at hearing the news we couldn't all agree on how to spend it. Joel and I insisted that we use $4000 to support four teachers. But Simon felt that paying teachers would polarize the older and younger people.

Joel argued that the money was given to us as "seed money" to ensure that we would become self-sufficient in the future. "We can't attract good people to work here unless we give them some financial security," he said. "The grant frees my time to help us find funds for next year. All of us who are being paid are responsible for keeping the project going."

Henry added that he would be unable to devote any time to

the school without financial support. He said that their baby, which Barbara would be having in the fall, would mean added food and hospital expenses. Reluctantly, Simon agreed that we should support teachers, and we voted to pay four teachers $1000 each.

We had decided to run a summer project for kids currently attending public schools. I felt it would be an ideal way for them to become acquainted with our project. Also, I saw it was a way to keep up our momentum, to spend our summer working as a group instead of letting our energies dissipate. The summer project helped us meet new people, who in turn recharged us with their own enthusiasm. Gil Mendelson, formerly a teacher in Montgomery County, had quite a few contacts with the dissident student groups in the county high schools. He helped us plan the summer project and recruit for it. Ruby Lerner, an undergraduate at Goucher College, had visited the school earlier in the year and now decided to spend the summer living and working with us. In mid-June she moved into our Jefferson Avenue house and lent her energy to everything from cooking to poetry, from contacting new students to Tarot readings. She helped us to set up our office over a nearby furniture store and organized our library in the attic. It was her enthusiasm and insanity that kept us sane during the summer.

Through a friend we met Dale Ostrander, a minister in the Cleveland Park area, who promptly offered us his church facilities for the summer. We did, however, have to go through a screening by the church board. One evening Reverend Ostrander called to ask me to meet the board the following afternoon to answer some of their questions.

The next day Evan and Carol came to see us about working at the school. They had come to Washington to investigate the possibility of jobs at Runaway House (an institution that feeds and protects kids who have run away from home). Someone there had sent them to Takoma Park to see us. Both had spent two years in the Peace Corps in Ethiopia and a year teaching in a black school in Mississippi. After three years working as "missionaries" to the "underprivileged" they wanted to return to the suburbs to confront their own middle-class backgrounds. The prospect of working with white suburban dropouts excited them. I hoped they would join us. They were interested in communal living, and as a couple could add stability to an adolescent commune.

In the midst of our conversation I remembered our meeting at the Cleveland Park church. Evan and Carol offered to drive me down there. The meeting was tense; I was groping for a way to explain the project without offending anyone. Most of the questions were not ideological. They were predictably mundane—"how much, how many" questions: Are you accredited? Do kids go on to college? Are you insured? Some of the better-informed members asked about drugs at the school. "We wouldn't want the place to become a hangout for bad types," someone added. I had expected the meeting to be like a cautious chess game—it turned out to be more like a tennis match.

Finally the meeting was over and a church member engaged Evan, Carol, and me in conversation. We told him we were about to find a place to eat. To our surprise he invited us to dinner. To his surprise we accepted. His wife was the most surprised of all, but she made the best of it. We sat down to dinner and began an uneasy conversation. After dinner our hostess took out some books on the order of "What to tell your child about God, Death, etc." I nodded and mm-hmmed, but Evan began arguing with her.

"Parents have no right to indoctrinate their kids," he said.

The lady became defensive. "I don't think this is indoctrination at all. It just helps to clarify questions that are puzzling to kids of that age."

"Sure, but you're 'clarifying' them with a definite point of view. Even if it's subtle, it's still indoctrination."

And so on. I didn't join the conversation. I thought pointless to argue about such basic beliefs, and I thought Evan resembled Harry Haller, the "Steppenwolf," an ungracious guest at the house of a bigoted professor. He argued humorlessly and self-righteously, more to convince himself than to convince the lady. But I liked Evan anyhow. He and Carol planned to travel for a few months and promised to return. I hoped they would.

As a result of the meeting, or possibly in spite of it, the church decided to let us use their facilities through the summer. We now had a core of about fifteen public high school students attending weekly meetings to plan classes and workshops. The new students listened rather passively as the resource people proposed and described classes. They still thought of us as a school, albeit a free school, where teachers would just be better entertainers. These kids brought with them a great deal of anxiety from public school. I thought that if we shared some activity or got to know each other in an informal setting, some of the tension we felt might be reduced.

We went on a retreat in the Shenandoahs, on the church mission site where we had spent some of our happiest moments the first year. The place was secluded—it could be reached only by a treacherous road. There were three or four stone buildings on the land, one of which could be heated if necessary.

It was the perfect time of year—insects were scarce and berries were plentiful. We made sassafras tea from the roots we picked; all of us slept on the wooden floor of the large building. The country had a relaxing effect on us. Almost unconsciously we slowed down. Even though a lot of us went on the trip, the open space allowed us a certain privacy. We felt a warm, silent bond as we shared the woods, the hills, the valleys.

I returned from the trip determined to carry over to our city existence the warmth of the past two days. I thought that some sort of "sensitivity group" would help us become closer to each other despite our physical dispersion and varied home scenes. At the same time I rejected the role of T-group leader. Kids were rightfully suspicious of the "impartial" shrink who diagnoses everyone else's problems but remains a mystery himself. I wanted to be part of a leaderless group, a "nexus" group where we would make the connections ourselves rather than rely on an outsider. I hoped to remove the mystique from psychology

—there is nothing magical about understanding people. I planned to begin by suggesting activities but hoped that the group would soon begin running itself.

At first so many people showed up that we found it nearly impossible to do anything in our small basement. We began with the usual face-touching and body-lifting. These were relaxing and fun, but they were still "exercises." They weren't spontaneous enough.

During one of our early classes a participant received a phone call from home. When she returned, obviously upset, many of us began to physically console her. We seized on what we thought was a chance to relate to a real emotion. But others in the group thought our reaction was contrived, a pretense to indulge ourselves. As a result a few people left the group.

Gradually the group became smaller and more hedonistic. Instead of challenging ourselves, we became fixated on those things that made us feel good. We spent one warm evening giving each other long, loving back massages to the tunes of Country Joe and the Fish. Yet we felt frustrated, because we couldn't move beyond this point. Later that evening we agreed on another retreat in the Shenandoahs, which we felt would be somewhat more satisfying than spending two nights a week in a dark basement.

The trip was awful. Those few of us who could make it just stayed overnight. The buildings had been burned down by some local crazies during a Fourth of July drunk. The mosquitoes were oppressive and so was the humidity. We were finally driven off the mountain by a helicopter spraying defoliant on the telephone poles.

After this the four or five people left in the group moved to the attic, where we could easily seal off our womb. I was upset, because we clung to each other and never really dealt with our problems. I felt impotent in the group because I, too, was unable to move beyond the "feelie" stage. Yet I realized that at that point the kids needed most to touch each other, even in an unreal environment. Like the summer project itself, this class helped people who had only nodded at each other in public school to feel part of a community.

After several weeks I realized that the experiences we shared were far more important than the classes. Some classes never even started, because no one was interested. Ruby's poetry class was valuable chiefly because she encouraged people to bring in their own poetry. When they read works of contemporary poets such as Ginsberg and Ferlinghetti or Ruby's former students, kids were able to relate the work to their own experience. "No matter how far off the subject we'd gotten," wrote one girl in the group, "someone always came back to something we'd read and added a different angle."

Most of those who participated in the project felt that it confronted them with a real alternative to public school. (A few of the kids in it subsequently left high school.) Carol Brown, one of the people most involved during the summer, had this impression:

> The individual groups did not make as much of an impression on me as the idea behind the whole thing. The summer turned into one huge philosophy class for me and, I think, a lot of others as well. It was a much more effective way to turn people on to the school than the meetings and retreats have been this year. The project really made it clear how standard schools inhibit people and discourage free learning (i.e., learning from each other rather than being under the control of one approved "teacher" and his ideas of what and how to learn). It also showed people how narrow the curricula are. For example, it turned me on to Hesse, and other people on to other things that public school wouldn't have, or things people hadn't tried because of grade averages, etc.

That summer we also talked about confronting the public school in a more direct fashion. Joel proposed that we organize an "alternative registration" on the day the Montgomery County public schools opened in the fall. He suggested that we prepare a leaflet with the help of activist students, and distribute it outside the schools. The leaflet would describe our project as a real alternative and would ask the students to join it. For a while we were very excited about this idea. Then we tried to determine the legal consequences of such an action. Would the schools call the police to stop us from illegally distributing leaflets on public property? But we didn't have enough time to plan it effectively, since it was already late in July. Joel and I were exhausted and wanted to get away for a month. Kathy would be leaving for England in early September. Monte spoke of traveling to California. That left Ruby, Simon, and Cookie as the only people who would be definitely living on Jefferson Avenue in August. And Simon, who was on probation, had natural qualms about taking part in an action that might get him arrested. We all agreed to postpone our leaflet until the coming fall, when we would be better organized. By that time we would have recruited a new group of students for the project who might want to get involved in an action like this. Gil felt that we should concentrate our energies in the fall on getting speaking engagements at local schools. Then, if the administrations refused to let us talk, we would have a perfect issue around which we could organize high school students.

2. Setting Things Up

While Joel and I were away during August, Ruby kept in touch with prospective students and arranged a parents' meeting for early September. I was supposed to run the meeting but I was reluctant. A month of California sunshine had hardly prepared me for the cold stares of overanxious parents. Worse than that, my dentist had put a bite plate in my mouth, and I sounded like Donald Duck.

I began the meeting by apologizing for my speech impediment and went on to describe the school as a place where kids could turn on rather than drop out, as a practical lesson in living, not a utopian experiment. I spoke of starting a newspaper in Takoma Park, of apprenticeships, of work within the Washington Free Community. Our students would speak to public high school assemblies and after-school clubs. "We're determined not to be an isolated experiment or a freak show," I said.

Then the parents began asking the predictable questions.

The first one who spoke asked if the school was accredited and whether students could go on to college after completing it.

I answered that we weren't accredited but all four of the kids who applied the first year were accepted at college. I explained that kids in the past had kept their own "logs" in which they described books they had read, conversations, other activities that influenced their thinking. When they felt ready to apply to college they converted their logs into transcripts. Then we helped them with their applications and recommendations.

Jeff's father added that Maryland public schools recognized our school as "legitimate," and the parent seemed satisfied. Questions continued in the same vein. Christine's father was still concerned that his daughter might not get into college. We reassured him that colleges used criteria other than high school grades. Pete's father wanted to know about drugs. We reassured him that we hadn't allowed drugs in the house in the past. Graham's mother asked about discipline. We assured her that the school would help kids develop self-discipline.

It was a reassuring evening for all of us. We had received an unusual amount of support from parents. Jeff's and Phil's parents donated their basements, Fred's father offered his legal services. I even had a friendly discussion with a parent who worked for the CIA. We felt more comfortable with parents, no longer afraid of them. A year's experience had taught us what they wanted to hear.

We didn't have too hard a time rationalizing our deceptiveness. Parents' concerns were often so far removed from those of their kids that we could respond only by calming their fears. We hoped that when they began to see their children grow they would become less anxious.

At the time we believed a lot of what we told the parents. We actually wanted the school to be more stable. After a year in which lethargic and destructive people had frequently set the tone for our house, we wanted to be more selective. Joel and I decided to "interview" prospective students—examine their motives for joining, find out their interests and expectations, and inform them of what we expected. After the first few interviews I realized the absurdity of this idea. When we told people what we expected, they nodded. What else could they do? Most people gave us the most idealistic reasons for joining the school, not because they were trying to deceive us but because they really expected to do wonderful things. I wasn't sure how I could predict which kids would benefit and which wouldn't. Cookie, for example, had seemed like the absolutely wrong person for the school. She was immature, uncommunicative, self-destructive. She didn't come to us on her own initiative—her parents brought her. Yet she made the most impressive gains of anyone. The school-commune was instrumental in her change. So I looked at the interviews as a mutual sizing up but hardly as a basis for exclusion.

We attributed a great part of our instability the first year to transience. Many new people who joined us in the spring became disappointed when they perceived nothing going on (i.e., no classes). Quite a bit was going on, but the new people were out of phase with those who had begun to work on their own. Perhaps if we let new people in only twice a year they could grow independent together.

Since we planned more than one commune, we realized that we couldn't rely on spontaneity to get things done as much as we had the first year. We remembered how well our group had worked together in May when we held meetings simply to coordinate what all of us were doing. Joel and I decided to institute a weekly school meeting this year at which the group could report progress, make decisions with a minimum of tiresome ideological discussion, and announce activities for the week.

Even in the organic atmosphere of the first year, a few people did most of the work. Now that we would be dispersed, it was more important to establish a means of sharing work and decisions. Joel and I didn't want to be bogged down as we had been in the past. Also, I wanted kids to emerge from their dependency, to feel that the project was their own. At the first meeting Joel and I proposed a rotating chairmanship for each meeting. The chairman would put together an agenda from written proposals submitted by members of the community.

"The reason for this formality," Joel explained "is to prepare people for the discussion, to give them time to collect their thoughts before they make the decision." In the past our meetings had lapsed into protracted discussions that frequently ended in a frustrating stalemate. Henceforth, we hoped, meetings would be "business meetings," short and to the point, which would free our time for more exciting things.

We tried to take on responsibility for every aspect of the project and became self-righteously annoyed when other members of the community didn't share our concern. When Evan and Carol first talked with us in June they had expressed interest in living communally with kids in the school. But when they returned in September, before they could really talk with the rest of us about it, they decided to move in with Henry and Barbara, who now were living in a small house on Spring Street in Silver Spring, Maryland. The four of them thought this would be a fine living situation, but their arrangement left the rest of us in a bind.

We had promised prospective students that they could live in communes if they wanted to and that we would help set them up. Since the law required an adult to sign the lease, and parents naturally wanted to be reassured that a "responsible adult" would be supervising their kids, we now had to find some other adults for the new commune. Joel was pissed off because Evan and Henry didn't feel this same responsibility.

Now it looked as if Mark Bezanson would have to move in with the new students. Mark was an old friend of Joel's and had spent the past two years in the Peace Corps. When we were looking for teachers in the spring Joel had proposed that Mark work full time at the school. Mark did not want to be the only adult in a house full of kids. We had to find someone to share the lease and other responsibilities. Henry suggested Herb, a fellow artist who was working part time and going to graduate school. Only Henry had met him before. We filled him in on the school, and he nodded intelligently, so we assumed he understood. The school was to pay his share of the rent in exchange for his signing the lease and living there. We hated to recruit teachers that way, but we felt that we had no choice.

Not surprisingly, after spending most of their lives in the sterile, monotonous suburbs, most of the new kids preferred to live in the city. Those of us who had survived the first year, on the other hand, had had our fill of city living. Finding a house downtown wasn't easy. One morning Mark, Joel, and I dressed up in our holiday outfits to visit a real estate agency on Columbia Road that was renting a large house. Joel told the woman in the office that we represented a school affiliated with the Friends' Meeting House. For good measure we threw in "foundation grant," "$10,000," "adult supervision." We were going along very well until she dropped the bomb. "Did you have a house on Park Road last year?"

We hemmed and hawed for a while but realized it was futile. She knew who we were. Our old landlord, she said, was angry about the damage the kids had done to the house. News travels fast in real estate circles.

After a few weeks of searching we found a house on Irving Street in Mount Pleasant which, ironically, was only a few blocks from our Park Road place. It was a roomy row house that faced Rock Creek Park, inconspicuous because it was above street level and obscured by trees. We told the landlady, a young German woman, about the school, and she was sympathetic.

Besides Mark and Herb, seven kids planned to live there, most of whom did not know each other. I hardly knew them either, but at first impression they were a rather diverse group. There was Harriet (18), who had been in our summer program. Physically and emotionally she was a "heavy" person— she carried a burden that she laid on everyone. She would introduce herself to people by sardonically talking about her days in the "nuthouse." Lucy (17) had straight, brown hair and a pleasant, expressive face. She had been on her own for a while and seemed much older than her age. I thought of Christine (15) as the stereotype teenybopper with long, curly blond hair and giggly sensuality. She appeared spoiled and immature, and even before moving into Irving Street she insisted that she could not get along with two of the other girls. Phyllis (17) was quiet and serious, had angular features and short brown hair.

I wondered what sort of energy lurked under her quiet exterior. Jeff (16) seemed to be a leader in the group. He had a wholesome brashness and resembled a long-haired Dwayne Hickman. Pete (15) had accompanied his father from San Diego. He and his family had been on the move all of his life. He was tall and thin, growing daily, but still he looked like a waif. Tom (17) had left home to avoid going to public school. His parents refused to support him, and he was looking for a job. When I met him he was trying to sell his motorcycle.

Meanwhile we had room for three new people at Jefferson Avenue but we were determined to be more selective about who would move in than we had in the past. One of the people who asked to move in was Allison, who came over one night with her mother. Joel got the impression that she would be using the place primarily to escape from her parents, and he thought she would add little to the household. The rest of us were turned off by a group of friends she brought over once. Joel strongly opposed her moving in, but I thought we should talk with her first and then decide.

I asked her whether she preferred her own apartment to a commune. She answered that she wanted to live in a commune so that she could meet more people.

"Right now, my parents let me come and go as I please. I usually spend a lot of time with my friends, but that's getting to be a drag. I'd like to get into something new."

With some embarrassment I told her of our misgivings about her friends and that we'd prefer they didn't come by too often. She agreed to this. I spoke to Allison a while longer about "communal responsibility" and so forth, and she still wanted to move in. We decided to give it a try.

We screened other people less carefully. I had never met Suzanne until she moved in—Joel had promised her a space weeks before. I only knew Fred slightly. He was a tall, gentle, quiet kid who seemed to want to apologize for living. He was the type of person who got along with everyone, so of course no one objected to his moving in.

Despite our rhetoric about everyone sharing in decision making, Joel and I tended to dominate things. Like mother hens, we clucked about, anxious to formalize the lessons we had learned, afraid of making new mistakes, constantly looking over everyone's shoulder.

At the second school meeting we discussed drugs. Joel, Mark, and I were becoming very paranoid. The police in Takoma Park had placed our house under surveillance, and three cops mysteriously appeared the day that kids moved into Irving Street. (They claimed to bo looking for someone who had committed a robbery in the area.) We felt that a bust at either house would destroy the whole school. By the night of the meeting, people at Irving Street had decided not to allow any drugs on the premises. They did feel, though, that anyone living there ought to be allowed to trip at the house.

I felt their decision might have serious repercussions for the rest of us. "Last year," I began, invoking the mythical tradition, "a kid at the school became very sick on acid, so sick we considered taking him to a hospital. Luckily he came out of it. But imagine what would have happened if we had to tell his parents?"

Most of the new people did not feel the issue was urgent. As far as they were concerned, the subject was "talked out"—they had nothing more to say. Some began drifting away, talking among themselves. Joel was speaking, and he had a hard time making himself heard above the noise; Christine was clinking coffee cups in the kitchen.

Joel stopped talking. "Look," he said, "it's impossible to speak with all this noise." Jeff muttered something about Joel being oppressive. Some kids defended Joel—everyone should be allowed to speak without being interrupted, they said. I said I hoped Jeff didn't equate being serious and wanting to speak without interruptions with being authoritarian.

Joel talked about the issue a few days later in his philosophy class. He was trying to explain the anarchists' concept of authority. The group had been reading selections from Kropotkin, Bakunin, Proudhon, Malatesta. Joel said that anarchism did not oppose rules and structure as such, but only those social arrangements that were imposed on people without their consent. Joel felt that many kids tossed the word "authoritarian" around much too loosely. They used it to label a person who expressed strong feelings that threatened them.

As "founders" of the school, Joel and I did have inordinate leverage. People felt that we two had invested so much of our egos in the school that we wouldn't listen to any criticism. At school meetings we made proposals that other people agreed to, and then assumed a consensus when there was none. Those who disagreed with our decisions simply ignored them.

In mid-October I suggested we spend a few days in small groups to figure out a better way to make decisions. Everyone said it was a good idea. But when we met the following week Henry and Simon tried to turn the gathering into a business meeting to discuss the purchase of a "school guitar." After a good deal of haggling the rest of us were able to break up into small groups. In one of these, Phyllis proposed that we vote on all issues rather than assume unanimity. I realized she was right—unanimity could only develop from the feeling that everyone had a vote of equal worth.

Even when we did vote on issues, kids felt intimidated. Late in the fall Simon proposed that the school pay him room and board plus a small stipend. He had single-handedly set up a leather workshop and had taught a few people some basic skills in leathercraft. But he felt his work had gone unrecognized and resented not being paid. I felt that although he had a skill to teach, he was not committed enough to helping other people. He had worked with only those people whom he felt comfortable with. He had refused to help Suzanne because he didn't like her. At the same time I realized that I was prejudiced against Simon's way of involving people, his style. Was this a basis for denying him support?

At the meeting Simon referred to things he had done in the past to justify support. Besides the leather shop he had helped Henry find the school a VW bus and get it registered. Joel asked him if he would be willing to take on other community responsibility in the future, such as driving people downtown.

"I don't know," said Simon. The group remained silent. Kids felt that Simon was asking us to reward him for what he had done in the past, just as Henry, Joel, and I had been re-

warded. Deep down they felt we should not support Simon—
they hardly had any contact with him. But they also felt that
the money wasn't theirs to spend anyway. They connected the
money with last year's program. It was last year's people who
had done the work to get the grant and who had already made
the major decisions about how to spend it. Reluctantly the
group voted to give Simon room and board and some spending
money. Only Evan voted against the proposal. "I have nothing
against Simon," he said. "I just don't think anyone should be
supported. We are letting ourselves be blackmailed."

During October we got our first bit of feedback on the school
when people from the first year began drifting back to D.C.
Greg and Dave felt that the school had become too dull and
too organized. "You know," said Greg, "I dug a lot of those
hassles we had last year. They may have been unpleasant, but
they were real, intense learning situations. I was talking with
Suzanne, and when I asked her how things were going, she
said, 'Oh, things are pretty well set until June.' "

I answered that things were more stable than last year but
quite a bit was going on. "Don't forget," I said, "these new
kids came into an already established project, and I'm sure
they expect some stability. But I think that in some ways they
are more mature than people last year, and they'll grow into
taking responsibility."

3. Classes

When Roger, another of the first-year students, returned for a
visit he ran into my room and shouted, "What's this I hear
about classes being compulsory this year?"

I calmed him down and told him we had no such rule. But I
could see how he'd gotten that impression. We had practically
handed out a course catalogue this year; each teacher had written a description of the courses he planned to teach. Unlike
the first year, when courses developed more organically, according to people's changing needs and interests, these classes
seemed already mapped out. Even though the teachers felt the

classes were flexible, we conveyed the feeling that everything
had been set up, that all an incoming student had to do was
find a comfortable niche.

We had been more thoughtful about classes this year because the school needed a focus. Now that we were spread out
among three communes across the city, classes had become our
common denominator. Many of our classes the first year
seemed fragmented and isolated. I looked forward to doing a
study that transcended traditional "disciplines" and that
would help kids to see themselves in historical perspective.
While reading *The Vanishing Adolescent,* by Edgar Friedenberg, I became intrigued by his analysis of the "silent generation"—the college students of the fifties. I wondered why students had changed in the past ten years from onlookers to
activists. I thought this question might be a good foundation
for a course. To answer it we would study every aspect of
American culture, politics, and economics during the fifties
and sixties.

I had prepared a reading list that included primary sources
on the fifties and sixties as well as commentaries by such
writers as Friedenberg, Jules Henry, David Riesman and Marshall McLuhan. I divided the readings into several categories.
At the first class meeting students decided they would pick one
book from each category. No one would necessarily be reading
the same book, but we would be covering approximately the
same area. I encouraged those kids who didn't want to do the
readings to start their own projects. I hoped that all people
would move beyond the planned readings into studies of their
own.

By the second week people had begun Jules Henry's *Culture
Against Man.* Although some felt the book was too "heavy,"
too difficult, they still were able to understand Henry's contention that society conditions us to want useless goods. I tried to
show them how, despite their "hip" life styles, they were still
consumers. Their affluent parents supported them, gave them
the money to buy clothes, records, dope. The group was sophisticated enough to see how the media manipulate the youth
market. They attacked a local "progressive" rock disc jockey

for being a phony. "He used to be a 'greaser,'" said one kid. They realized he was mainly out to sell things, including himself; his hipness was a pretense, a commodity.

But, as I realized, there was some danger in providing people with a ready-made learning situation. In my class I began to act more like a traditional teacher. The kids wanted me to be like an entertaining college lecturer, and I complied. I found that they were not doing the readings. "Maybe we would do the readings if you gave us an actual assignment," one kid said quite seriously. One day Graham said there was no unity to the course, because we all were reading different books. In response I drew up a list of broad questions that I hoped would help them focus their individual work. But I realized the class was moving entirely in the wrong direction.

Other classes were also floundering. Evan had begun an ecology group in September. The class had been spurred by a visit from Barry Weisberg, a radical ecologist from the West Coast, but fell apart when people had to do work on their own. At first Evan did much of the research and brought in most of the material for the class. He began to feel that other people weren't interested enough to follow up the work on their own. Sometimes people agreed on a time and place to meet and only one or two showed up. Evan was justifiably annoyed. "If you don't want to be in the class," he said at one meeting, "don't pretend that you do."

For a while the ecology "group" consisted of Evan and Phyllis. Both were dissatisfied with the way the school was being run. Why emphasize classes, they said, if they only mirror the relationships of public school? Evan resented the assumption that teachers should "fill kids up like little vessels" until they were full of information. Phyllis had decided that no school at all was better than this one. She had learned how to learn on her own and came to resource people with a real interest, not just to take up time. Too many people in the school, she felt, were just going through the motions. They were neither learning anything nor growing closer to each other.

Evan complained that Joel and I spent so much time organizing that we were out of touch with what really was going on.

Joel suggested that we have a meeting to discuss why some classes were failing. Besides Joel and me, Evan, Phil, Phyllis, and Suzanne showed up. Phyllis told us that now that she was doing work on her own she could find nothing at the school that was worthwhile.

"Maybe other people in the school who aren't as 'together' as Phyllis might benefit from classes and other organized activity," I suggested. "It might help them find something that they really want to get into."

"Not if they are passive in these activities," Evan said. "I'm really beginning to believe that it is impossible to teach, as such."

Joel disagreed. "When the school first started I had been influenced by Carl Rogers, who suggested the same thing. But after my philosophy class floundered for a while the first year, I realized there has to be someone in the group who can bring the discussion into focus."

Joel had spent the past few months teaching at a junior college. This teaching situation had been "structured" in the sense that Joel had organized a curriculum and frequently lectured. Yet he found the class rewarding because the students were older, more diverse, and more "curious" than our high-school-age people. Joel thought a class was valuable provided people were interested in the subject matter.

Suzanne agreed. She thought some classes had failed because the teachers involved did not provide enough structure at the beginning, when kids were just getting involved and didn't know much about the subject matter anyway.

"Right now," Evan answered, "I don't think I want to teach that way. I prefer a study group approach. Don't forget, I knew as little as anyone else when we began the ecology class—it's just that people looked at me as someone who would do most of the work. I was perfectly willing to do my share, but apparently others weren't. But that's not the point. The real point is that we have no sense that we are a community other than our money and our classes—our 'official school activities.' Why can't we just come together and talk and be with each other—talk about anything?"

This hadn't been much of a problem the first year. Since we all stayed around the big house, discussions could go on all the time. But now nobody knew what the "hub" of the school was—it certainly wasn't the Friends' Meeting House. Outsiders felt uncomfortable at the communes. I spent little time at Irving Street and hardly knew the people there. But we realized that classes could hardly be the focus of the school.

4. Development of the Communes

Takoma Park, Maryland, is an unusual community. It is a small town in an area of sprawling, commercial suburbs which has its own government (a mayor and council). It was founded in the late nineteenth century, primarily by white middle-class Protestants who built large, substantial homes (many of which are now subdivided into apartments). It became the international headquarters of the Seventh-day Adventist Church and the seat of its foremost educational institution, Columbia Union College. Many of the stores on Carroll Avenue, the town's main street, close on Saturday in observation of the sabbath. And the town's best restaurant, the Electric Maid, sells vegetarian food and has a bakery that prepares pastries made without chemicals or the usual preservatives. The law forbids the sale of alcohol in the Montgomery County section of Takoma Park (the town extends into the District of Columbia, Montgomery County, and Prince George's County).

The social composition of the town has changed radically in the last several years. Blacks, Spanish-speaking people (many of them from Cuba), and Appalachians have moved to the Sylvan Oasis (or the Azalea City, as it is sometimes called). Hippies have started communes in the large houses, the best-known of which is called Toad Hall. As the population of the town increased, developers built a large number of high-rise apartments. From our woody, almost rural perch on Jefferson Avenue we could see Maple Avenue below us, dotted with towering apartment buildings. There were luxury and middle-income dwellings, and there was the Winchester-Takoma, a brick building that had predominantly black tenants.

Takoma Park was becoming a "gray area," wedged in between the District of Columbia and the more prosperous suburb of Silver Spring. It had the classic problems that afflict lower-middle-class communities—crowded schools, high food prices, rising taxes, spiraling land costs, increasing crime. Sometimes people were able to organize to stop the planning that was supposedly done in their own interest. A group of activist citizens had defeated the plan to have the North Central Freeway run through Takoma Park.

When we moved into our house on Jefferson Avenue in June we vowed not to make the same mistakes we had made in Mount Pleasant. We would meet our neighbors immediately, in order to overcome their initial suspicions, and would try to find a way to relate the problems they were facing. Lower-middle-class families, many of whom owned their own homes, lived on our block. There were also a good number of people living there who had moved from Appalachia and had jobs as construction workers, carpenters, gas station attendants, and mechanics.

We had great intentions but had a hard time overcoming our hesitancy about meeting people in the neighborhood. A few younger guys—three junior high school students and a fellow in his twenties who was working as a carpenter—sought us out and we became quite friendly. They were all from Appalachia. In the minds of the others living on the block our isolation must have reinforced their stereotypes about long-haired kids. Our home became an object of intense curiosity. The large red peace symbol painted on the door enhanced our visibility.

The man who owned the house next door imagined the worst about us. He thought we were running a dope den (later in the year he called the house a youth hostel) and warned his children to stay away. He must have communicated his fears to the authorities, because several weeks after we arrived a housing inspector came to check the place.

When he rang the doorbell he woke up most of us. When some of the kids came to the door dressed in bathrobes and nightgowns and saw who it was, they scattered—in his eyes a sure confession of sin. I came out to talk to him. The house had been illegally occupied by three families—it was a one-family house—and he was checking to see if any violations of the code still existed.

"How many people live here? "Five," I lied. I remembered hearing that five or fewer unrelated people constituted a family. "What are all these names doing on the mailbox?" he asked me. I explained that we had recently moved from a place where many people lived—they were traveling and had no addresses. My explanation did not satisfy him. Later we heard that he considered the kids' bleary eyes an obvious sign that they were taking drugs.

A few days later the mailman refused to deliver a check to me because he claimed my name wasn't on the mailbox. I went running down to the post office and made a fuss. The postmaster insisted he couldn't hand the check to me over the counter. When I protested that I had no other money, he agreed to deliver it personally. Then he gave us a tip: if we left only one of our three mailboxes up, the post office would deliver all mail and we would not have to list our names.

We girded ourselves for a long struggle—we expected to be evicted. We were determined not to sit passively in the face of harassment, as we had done in Mount Pleasant and on Madison Street. (We describe our response to the threat of eviction in detail in Chapter VI.) But the crisis blew over. Later we learned that an official of the zoning board had circulated a petition on our block to oust us from the neighborhood. Only the apathy of our neighbors, who refused to sign, prevented him from succeeding.

Then, in the early fall, the police began to pester us. The Takoma police, whom a local lawyer called the Keystone Kops, began parking conspicuously near the house. A squad car would sit there for five or ten minutes and then drive away. They also began copying down license numbers and giving us tickets for illegal parking.

Our relationship with the younger kids in the neighborhood was also becoming tense. We were so happy to have some ties with the community that we encouraged them to use our house whenever they wanted. During the summer they helped Ruby clean up and do other things around the house. They became friendly with Simon, who taught them the guitar and involved them in building the leather shop in our basement. But sometimes they made me uptight. Once they brought some beer to our house, got drunk, and began fighting with each other. I didn't want this kind of thing happening in our house and asked them to leave. One of the guys was so spaced out that we had to escort him home.

Then one day we left them alone in the house and returned to find some money missing. I thought they might have taken it, so we talked to them the next day. They said that they suspected a young neighborhood kid of stealing the money—they had seen him hanging around the house. I didn't really believe them, but I decided to let it ride.

One day Fred flashed some money he had recently earned in front of the kids. He left for the evening, and sure enough, next morning the money was gone. I knew they had taken it this time because no one else had access to Fred's room. I got really upset and wanted to confront the kids the next day. But Joel felt that Fred should take the initiative. And he added, "You shouldn't do anything rash, because I think it's important to have them as friends."

"There isn't any friendship," I shouted. "They're just taking advantage of us—I can't see this as a basis for friendship."

"Well, look at their impression of us," Joel continued. "Where do we get our money from? We've been to college, but we don't work—they don't see the school as 'work.' We always have these cars around. And all our broken record players— We're so casual about things of great importance to these kids, it's no wonder they want to take advantage of us.

"Not only that, but we were good liberals. We let them in out of a feeling of duty, we were too condescending and too patronizing. We never really made them feel part of a community. I mean, when they would come over, we would just stop whatever we were doing and entertain them. Maybe if we treated them more realistically they wouldn't have felt that we were using them or bullshitting them."

We eventually did talk to the two boys and tried to explain that we did not have money to throw away. But it was too late to repair a relationship damaged through mutual exploitation. From mid-October on, we saw little of the kids and spent less and less time in our neighborhood.

Meanwhile we were having great difficulty living together. Simon and I found our differences intolerable. One night about 4:00 A.M. I awoke to the sound of Simon and some friends "jamming" in the basement. I was up on the second floor, but I could feel their loud, electronic music vibrating through the house. I staggered to the landing. "Will you shut the fuck up?" I yelled.

Grudgingly they lowered the music. I made a note to discuss it rationally in the morning, but I realized we couldn't mediate such basic differences. Literally, we were as different as day and night.

In November a conflict of another sort arose. Simon wanted to be able to use drugs in the house. Joel and I adamantly opposed him. We had signed the lease and refused to be responsible for someone else's transgressions.

"How can we be 'equals' if you keep using the 'lease' as veto power?" Simon asked.

He was right. As long as the older people had greater power (and also took greater risks), adolescent-adult communes would fall apart.

Both Joel and I began to get restless at Jefferson Avenue. Neither of us had established satisfactory relations with the new people in the house. At first I had felt attracted to Suzanne, turned on by her poetry, her hard softness. But as soon as I showed interest, she closed up. Angrily I realized I had been seduced, and hated her for it. Even after my original resentment wore off, we lived in constant tension. We knew exactly how to make each other angry.

Possibly because he was so unobtrusive, Fred and I got along fine. Predictably, Allison was away much of the time. Thus there was no buffer to absorb the tension between Suzanne and me. One night Suzanne had a music lesson at seven o'clock and asked me to drive her to her teacher's. I agreed reluctantly. On the way there she kept telling me how selfish I was for not wanting to drive her.

"Well, it's an inconvenience for me to rush through dinner," I said.

"This teacher is something special, and I have to make it when *she* wants me to," Suzanne said.

When I returned home Allison gave me a message: "Suzanne is angry. She arrived too late for the appointment. She said to tell you to pick her up."

"*Tell* me? Tell me, shit. Let her hitch home."

I flatly refused to pick her up, so finally Simon did. Still, I was fed up with the whole situation and decided to speak with Joel.

"I think this stuff is inevitable when you live with kids," he said.

"What do you mean?"

"Well, when they ask childish, unreasonable things, you find yourself acting like them. I'm convinced that I can't live with kids anymore. They can't help me with my problems. I don't feel that I've been growing this year."

I told Joel I could no longer live with Simon or Suzanne. We spoke seriously of leaving the Jefferson house to the school and finding a commune with other adults.

Irving Street also was having problems. By the end of November Mark was ready to leave. The noise and disorder were an ordeal for him, especially because he had nowhere to escape to except his room. Unlike Joel, who could leave to visit friends in D.C., Mark knew few people in the area. He had joined the school as Joel's friend, but his experience was so different from Joel's that they could hardly communicate. Mark left suddenly in December. He was in such a hurry that he didn't have time to explain it to his classes.

Phyllis and Lucy were also dissatisfied with life at Irving Street. People living there hadn't particularly chosen to live with each other. They were just thrown together. The people who were least willing to work set the tone for the rest of the house. The place was quickly becoming a hangout. Lucy and Phyllis felt that there wasn't enough going on at the school to warrant staying in the area. They spoke of hitching to California and perhaps staying there for good.

"Fine," I said. "If you've found something you'd rather do, go ahead and do it. To me this means your time here has been valuable, because you've found some direction. But don't put down the school. Just because it isn't right for you, that doesn't mean it isn't worthwhile for some people."

"Look," Lucy said, "we don't have to apologize or rationalize to anybody if we are going to leave." She must have sensed I hadn't really meant what I said. I still had too much of my ego invested in the project. I had interpreted what they were saying as a criticism of the school, and hence, of myself.

Ever since the beginning of October Evan and Carol had talked about moving out of Henry and Barbara's house. They had never felt that it was their own place. Irving Street was disintegrating, and Lucy, Pete, Phyllis, and Jeff also thought about finding their own house. Suzanne and Fred wanted a more intense living situation than Jefferson Avenue provided. They also had never felt at home at "our" commune. The six kids plus Evan and Carol teamed up to find a house.

Shortly before Christmas the eight of them found a house on Madison Street, several blocks from where we had rented our first place a year before. It was an old house with a shabby wooden porch, cracked, fragile walls, and a leak in the attic. The kids shared two bedrooms, Evan and Carol the third. Everyone slept on mattresses on the floor. The living room furniture consisted of one table (formerly a door), a womblike wicker chair, and other assorted broken chairs. They patched up the attic and turned it into a library-community room.

Simon, Cookie, and Allison also moved out of Jefferson— Simon and Cookie to their own apartment, Allison to the house of some friends. I felt that this was a change for the better. Living with Simon made it impossible for me to relate to him on any other level. When I visited Simon and Cookie in their new apartment I was pleasantly surprised. Compared with their quarters at Jefferson Avenue and at Park Road, it was immaculate. They had finally trained Puppy, their dog, to shit outside. They were living in a two-family house and had become friendly with their neighbors, a lady and her teen-aged daughter. They often baby-sat for the lady's younger kids or cooked dinner together.

I felt a lot more respect and affection for them now that we lived separately. It was a sign of strength that we could accept life-style differences, live in separate houses, yet still remain part of the same community. I wondered what would have happened the previous year if Arthur, Bill, and Alice had set up their own household, yet still remained part of the school.

5. *School or Community?*

I was very optimistic about the new Madison Street house. All of the people there had lived communally before and had chosen to live together this time. Not only did they share work but they shared their personal conflicts. When Phyllis and Suzanne had trouble getting along, the entire household met to help them solve their problems. This was in strong contrast to Jefferson Avenue, where the group had never dealt with the strong animosity between Suzanne and me.

Visitors came away from Madison Street feeling the energy and enthusiasm of the group. I stayed there for a few days in January. I remember sitting on a rug in their cozy attic, quietly talking, listening to music, smoking hash. I thought of their place as a warm oasis in the chilly, gray Washington winter. It reminded me of our old Madison Street house. Kids at both places had little need to attend classes at the school, because they had all of the resources and reinforcement they needed at home. When Phyllis became interested in visiting Cuba, she began studying Spanish on her own. For a few months everything at the house was labeled in Spanish. Although the group often chose not to become involved in school activities, they opened themselves up to the city. They attended weekly Women's Liberation workshops and became involved with all kinds of political activity. They even organized their own course, a study group on political economy.

In February they began working with the "D.C. Nine," a group of priests and nuns on trial for destroying Dow Chemical files. During the week and a half the trial lasted, the Madison Street people spent their days at the courthouse, their nights at St. Stephen's church rapping with the defendants. The trial began on a Friday, and through some oversight the kids and Evan were admitted to the courtroom. When the judge warned that the Vietnam war was not an issue in the trial and refused to admit any testimony that included the word "Vietnam," Evan stood up and shouted at him.

As the guards moved to oust him from the courtroom Jeff blocked the way. Both were removed from the courtroom but were not cited for contempt. Later on in the week the defense counsel and a few of the defendants did receive contempt citations. Madison Street, along with the D.C. Nine, learned that the courtroom could hardly be a forum for political questions. The nine were, predictably, found guilty, and unfortunately were prevented from publicly explaining much of their behavior.

The strong spirit at Madison Street made the rest of us more aware of how little we shared as a community. In January we began having "community dinners." We usually held them weekly, alternately at Jefferson, Irving Street, Madison Street, and Gil's house. Everyone brought some kind of dish or drink, and we usually had a loud, musical time. But this type of activity hardly made us a community, especially when we did so little together the rest of the week.

There were other experiences—such as a trip to hear Allen Ginsberg—when our school became a community. A large group of us went to Baltimore to hear him read at Goucher College. Ruby was to introduce him and had promised us all free admission. When we got there we couldn't locate Ruby, so Jeff, Lucy, Pete, and I sneaked into an empty projection booth. But before the reading was half over, a guard discovered us. We were ushered into a small room where a hundred or so other people were listening to the reading over a scratchy public-address system. Ginsberg stopped the reading and refused to continue until everyone was allowed into the auditorium.

Goucher was the wrong place for Ginsberg. He bared his homosexual soul and found neither empathy nor compassion. As he commanded his "Master" to perform various acts with him, as he became more explicit, I felt the audience tighten. His openness drove people away from understanding. At one point I thought the audience was about to titter, but I realized they were too uptight to do even that.

Later we went to a strange, crowded party for Ginsberg where people crowded around the poet, or talked of gathering around the poet. He approached Jeff and Suzanne.

"Are you two sleeping together?" he asked.

Suzanne shrugged coyly. "No," said Jeff.

The sangría began to take effect. We heard some music in the other room and began dancing to the Band. I remember Ginsberg dancing to "Rag Mama Rag" as we erupted in alcoholic frenzy.

During the November moratorium we came out of our cocoons to talk with high school students from Montgomery Country at an all-day conference we organized at a local church. Several hundred kids streamed in and out during the day to listen to talks on ecology and the economics of U.S. imperialism, to attend workshops on Cuba, North Vietnam, high school organizing, to pick up literature, and just to sit and rap. Phyllis was so excited by the discussion on Cuba that she began thinking of joining one of the Venceremos brigades.

Despite these experiences, we painfully lacked the ardor and excitement that had welded us together the year before. Joel felt the differences most keenly. He increasingly became identified with the role of "organizer" now that the relationships between all of us had become more formal. The school became abstract to him, no longer exciting and satisfying. Late in January he decided, not without some guilt, to take a trip to the West Coast. When he left he wrote us all a letter:

Dear Friends,

This is to let you know that I have decided to leave Washington for several months. I have a great many mixed feelings about doing this, for I love you all tremendously. We have shared in creating an exciting social experiment—an association which I will never forget. Yet this is something I must do. The decision is not sudden but has been brewing in my head since before the holiday. I have found that after two years of involvement with the project I have grown stale and have found it hard to generate my old enthusiasm. Moreover, I have been so heavily engaged in organizational work, in teaching, etc. that I have failed to take care of many personal priorities. I need a chance to be totally free of responsibilities, a chance to get some perspective, to pull the loose threads of my life together. I have postponed dealing with my personal needs for too long. To do so any longer would be unfair to myself and you.

I really hope that our relationship does not end with my departure. It would be impossible to find as beautiful a group of people as all of you. I am sure our lives will intersect, that we will build a new world together.

Love,
Joel

To the Madison St. Commune,

I wish you especially good luck, for you are beginning to create a tender and warm community that will serve as a contagious example for all of us.

After Joel's departure I became more and more the spokesman for the school. One night, on a visit to Madison Street, Evan and I began to discuss the school structure. Evan insisted that people came to meetings only to hustle money for themselves. "The school doesn't really exist," he said, "except for the structure which you're hung up on. To me the school is just the people, and I don't need the school to be with them or to help them. The whole corporation ought to be disbanded and we should start over again."

I got really defensive. "What do you mean, the school does nothing? The school found Joanne a potter to work with and a metal sculptor for Mary. It gives people the chance to do what they want to do, and they even get credit for it if they want to go to college. And the school's money has been used for the film classes and to help support people—"

Evan: "That's it, right there. Only the money can hold peo-

ple together—just this big 'tit.' As for the other stuff, it was Gil
who found the potter for Joanne. And the trouble with doing
one thing and telling parents and colleges another is that you
begin to believe your own rhetoric. You tell parents and prospective students about all the classes that are going on. You
name activities, and therefore they become worthwhile. You
know as well as I do that's bullshit. Classes aren't the most
important thing going on here."

I: "Well, so what if money is an important thing? We had
enough of a survival trip last year. Now we have the time to do
other things. Why shouldn't money be a rallying point?"

Evan: "Because it's not their own. Because it was spent before any of them came here. Because it's been wasted! How
much money have we spent on bullshit? The office, for example? Or supporting people who have done nothing? It's too late
to change that relationship now. Since kids think that there is
an endless flow of money, it doesn't matter to them how it's
spent. That's how Simon convinced the school into providing
him with support. But now that our endless supply seems to be
running out, how are we going to deal with it? I suggest we
stop support and put a freeze on all checks. Maybe then we can
begin to talk about 'community.' "

I: "But maybe some kids don't want to be in a community
or aren't ready to be in one. Like Graham said, 'I don't care
how you spend the money—it isn't mine, it's my mother's, and
I don't want to be bothered with it.' He knows what he wants
to do and how he wants to spend his time, but he doesn't seem
to be interested in the school as a community. Most of the kids
who live at home have different needs right now from those of
the people who are living at Madison Street. Kids at Madison
Street no longer need the school, because they have outgrown
it. You don't need classes if you have reinforcement all the
time. But the kids living at home don't have the opportunity
for contact that the commune kids do. They want us to set up
classes and activities for them. That's what a school is. It's the
responsibility of the older people to set up these things, and
I'm not going to argue about whether Gil acted as Gil or as the
'school' when he got Joanne an apprenticeship."

Evan: "Don't you see that's a self-fulfilling prophecy? If you make most of the important decisions for people because you feel they can't or don't want to make them for themselves, you're still depriving them of the opportunity to learn how. They start thinking that they can't make any decisions, and they don't try. It's a vicious circle."

I: "But it is a fact that the school is transient; people are changing constantly, and many of us may be leaving at the end of the year. It was the school that originally brought Madison Street together—now they have a community of their own. I think that's a good thing."

Evan: "Why are you setting us apart from the rest of the kids? We are still a part of the community. The point is that a community is possible with all of the people in the school. That's better than lying to ourselves and indulging the kids the way their parents do. As far as I am concerned, the school is an artificial structure. It doesn't exist."

I: "Look, I don't think we're communicating."

Evan: "We're communicating very well. It's just that to you communication means proving that you're right."

I was very upset when I returned home that evening. I knew that I had resisted Evan's arguments so vehemently only because they were largely valid. If we were paying teachers to ensure their commitment to the project, why were three of those who had been paid no longer involved? Mark had left the school in December, Joel had left a month later for an indefinite period, and Henry was only a ghost, a signature that appeared on school checks.

Still, I wasn't ready to abandon the school structure entirely, as Evan has suggested. I thought it foolish to force a "community" on people when they really were looking for something else. Graham and Chris, for example, preferred to spend their time studying music rather than wrestling with communal problems. When they joined the school they could have been part of a commune, but they consciously chose not to be. I saw myself as representing the "commuter" kids, who wanted some kind of contact and reinforcement without a totally absorbing living situation.

The education class I ran that spring served primarily to give me a chance to talk with the kids who didn't live in communes. In March we invited Alex Rode to speak to us. He had run an experimental high school in D.C. for five years, before these projects became fashionable. The kids in his school had their own apartments, worked during the day, and had classes at night. Most of them stayed with the school for the full time that it operated—a remarkable accomplishment in the light of our own transience. They all took the same courses at the same time. After a couple of months they changed the courses. The courses were not required, yet everybody took part in them. They had a house in which the school activities took place, but nobody lived there.

"Fixing up a house of your own can really give you a sense of being together," Alex said. "That was one of the most important things we did."

Mary expressed what all of us must have been thinking while we listened to Alex: "Why don't we get a place for the commuter people? No one would live there, but whoever wanted to stay there could stay temporarily. It would be a place of our own."

Pam, another student who lived at home, was also excited by the idea, because she never really felt at home at any of the communes. For the rest of the afternoon Alex did very little talking. But he had been the catalyst for one of the most exciting discussions we had all year. Audrey and I spent the next afternoon looking for a house, but without success. Then we thought about using Henry's old place in Silver Spring which was now unoccupied. It was located in a commercially zoned area, where we could get away with making noise and having a lot of people around. During the next couple of weeks we began to put the place in shape. We vacuumed the living room carpet repeatedly and scrubbed the kitchen. We moved our library out of the Jefferson Avenue attic and into Spring Street. Matt put our adding machines, stationery, checkbooks into a closet in one of the bedrooms and labeled it "Office." We decided not to install a phone so that we could have more comfort and privacy.

The idea of a "commuter house" excited me. I had hoped people would just hang out there, talk, do things with each other. I expected that projects would evolve naturally from this more informal contact. Yet people used the place infrequently except for our "formal" get-togethers, such as meetings, classes, and dinners. Only Matt spent much time there—probably because he had access to a car. Mary lived in southeast Washington, too far away to just drop over. I realized how so much of our lack of community was due to physical dispersion.

I also struggled with Evan's contention that we misrepresented the school to parents. When we held another parents' meeting in the spring I emphasized the importance of the school as a place where kids could find their own direction. I was still into "listing" the activities going on, but I also said that the new commuter house was simply a place to "be."

After a while the same questions cropped up. "If you people are going to build a new society," Matt's father asked, "where will the kids get the skills and knowledge to do it? Your school doesn't offer science and things of that sort. They all can't become candlemakers, you know."

I explained that people in the school were in a period of reaction at the moment and would probably move on to another stage. "Kids here are coming from a school system that emphasizes science inordinately. They see technicians as people who have no morality of their own, who do research without understanding the implications of their work. So kids are not reacting against science but against the phony 'neutrality' of technology. There are some kids at the school who are interested in biology and architecture. I'm certain when they get into these things more deeply, or if they decide to undertake a career in science, they will have a better perspective than those kids in 'science-oriented' schools."

"Well, then, what can we do for our kids?" one father asked.

"You can leave them alone," Evan answered. "Don't support them financially and don't hassle them."

"How do you mean 'hassle'?"

"What you've been doing," Evan replied, "—asking your

daughter to do things your way, to change her life style. I've hardly met any parents who accept the way their children are. I don't mean they have to live the way their kids live or even like it. Just accept it and not try to change it. I remember one day some parents were visiting Madison Street, and as I walked in from the street I could feel the heaviness and hostility in the air. Not all of it was spoken, but it was there just the same."

"Do you mean us?" asked Phyllis' mother.

"No," Evan said. "It was some other people."

It had been some other people, but many of the parents there began to feel upset and defensive. Evan continued: "I would like to have some parents visit with us, just to watch and learn, although I know I wouldn't feel comfortable—the only parents here with whom I can feel comfortable are Fred's parents. They don't like many of the things he does, but they see how futile it is to exert their own wills on him."

One father in particular became angry. "What do you mean you wouldn't feel comfortable with me? Maybe I wouldn't feel comfortable with you either. You won't make me feel any more welcome by being so self-righteous and condescending about child-rearing. It's much easier to talk about what you would do than to actually be faced with the responsibility of having a child."

"Wait a minute," Evan said. "I'm not condemning you. If I was a father, I don't know how different I would be. It's just that parents are taught that kids are their property. That's a difficult premise to extract yourself from. But Fred's parents, at least, are trying."

For the first time we were honest with most of these parents, and it felt good. We hit upon the crux of the school—helping kids to leave home and lead lives of their own. Other things came out at the meeting. Cynthia's father asked about drugs. I said that I was sure kids were involved with drugs to some extent, just as they were before they got to the school. "The only rules we have are against drugs on school premises—as a legal precaution. I'm sure these rules have been broken. But don't expect me to say that I enforce them or that I think that all drugs are harmful. I have my own opinion about which drugs are bad. If I see someone getting into a destructive drug thing I talk to him about it—but not as some authority figure who is telling him what to do. That's futile."

This was followed by silence. There was nothing more to be said about drugs. The meeting had been a shock to most of the parents. They hadn't been reassured, as in the past. I'm sure some of the parents wanted to hear, "There are no drugs here," even though they knew that there were. Or that classes were going and their kids would surely be going to college. Not all the parents felt cheated. Joanne's mother said that she was glad that there had been a preliminary communication between the school and the parents. She suggested that we continue these meetings in smaller groups with kids, parents, and teachers. I mentioned this idea to a lot of parents and suggested they contact her. No one ever did.

During this period, I chose to ignore Evan's suggestions about abolishing support. But in March, Matt, who had been keeping the books, reported that our funds were unusually low. If we didn't cut back on something quickly, we would run out before June. Jeff suggested we get rid of the office we had been renting since the summer. "No one ever uses it—nobody's there to answer the phone. What a waste of money!"

I objected that we needed an "official address." "We can use the Friends' Meeting House," Evan said, and Jeff's motion passed. Once again Evan insisted we abolish support.

The group set up a committee—which consisted of Gil, Matt, two other people, and myself—to examine our old budget and propose a new one. When we met we decided to spend no more money without the approval of all the people in the community. The committee also felt the time had come to withdraw support from Henry and Simon (Mark and Joel no longer collected money). Withdrawing support was difficult in a community so concerned with justice and resentful of "authority." Yet many of us felt Henry and Simon were absorbing money that could be spent for better purposes—for example, renting the commuter house. Henry was so preoccupied with his own work that he had no time for the kids. Simon had taught leathercrafts to a few people, but he ignored everyone else. Still, I was unsure of how I felt. Both Henry and Simon had something to offer if people approached them—and perhaps this was the best way to learn. But most kids in the school wanted adults who would spark their excitement and provide guidance.

On the following day we presented our budget changes to the rest of the group. Much of the meeting was spent discussing trivia. By the time we made our presentation, only a handful of people were left to make the major decision—whether or not we should continue to support Henry and Simon. Many of the kids there, primarily commuters, were surprisingly adamant about cutting off support. Yet they found it hard to actually make the decision. Someone proposed that we extend Henry's salary an extra month, and the motion passed. I thought this was a cop-out. Simon wanted a loan to purchase more leather which he said he would repay from the sales of the finished products. We all agreed to this proposal. I thought this was the ideal way to use the foundation money.

I realized that we had set a bad precedent in the fall. The first year we supported everyone. The school had very little money, but what we had was communal. School funds paid for food and rent, bought gasoline for our cars, supported kids who couldn't have lived there otherwise. We supported Simon and Henry because they were members of the community, not because of any special role they played. Henry's personality hadn't changed in a year, but my feelings about him had. The first year we were close friends. Now I saw him—and judged him—only in terms of what he was doing for the school.

I had become self-righteous about my own involvement in the project. I remembered the time a few months earlier when Henry had asked to borrow the bus to take Barbara for a Monday morning checkup. That particular Sunday night I was using the bus to pick up a girl friend. I told Henry I'd drive it over in the morning.

"I'd rather you did it now," he said, "because I won't have time to drive you home then."

I said that I would hitch, and he agreed. But a few hours later he showed up in Takoma Park and demanded the bus.

"The bus isn't only yours! You act as if you own it, and I'm getting sick of that crap!"

"Well that's too fucking bad," I said. "I drove a bunch of school people to a rock concert in Georgetown before making my social call tonight. I use the bus to ferry people back and forth all week. If you want to use it more, why don't you do more of the communal driving too?"

Even if I was right, I was addressing Henry as if he were a lazy employee rather than a fellow member of the community. I saw how being a "director" dehumanized me, and I no longer wanted to play that role. I had finally accepted Evan's analysis.

At the next meeting I proposed abolishing support for all teachers. My turnabout took quite a few kids by surprise. They saw it as an abdication, an abandonment of the school. "Why wasn't all this settled in September?" Chris shouted, echoing all of the confusion and frustration that had characterized our group life for so many months. Herb also protested that this violated the agreement we had made in September. He had a valid point. But we had had our fill of his whiny selfishness. He had contributed so little to Irving Street or the school that we ignored his objections entirely.

Evan proposed that we support everybody at all the houses who needed money, provided we found ways to raise money first. He felt that we had to build a community together before we could take from it. Herb still insisted he be paid even if he didn't help with fund raising. "Irving Street needs money now," he said. "Two people have moved out, which means we're minus seventy dollars each."

"We need money at Madison too," Evan answered. "But we won't take from the school unless we're putting money back."

"But who knows if we can raise any money now?" Herb asked.

I had this doubt myself, but I was ready to try. Anything was better than continuing our double standard of support.

We had done very little fund raising in the past. Matt Clarke, Tom, Lucy, and I delivered phone books in October. This venture didn't net us much cash, but it showed us that shitwork done communally with a goal in mind could be fun.

Linda, and Jack—frequently stayed overnight. Second-year commuters felt little attachment to the communes, perhaps because no one commune was the hub of activities. But many were not prepared to make the break with their families. Only one day student, Pam, considered moving into a commune. In March she spoke of moving to Madison Street but backed off because she didn't feel ready for the intensity of communal life.

In January, Madison Street appeared to be the most dynamic part of the school. The kids showed a great deal of autonomy in setting up the commune; the first months were marked by a hard-working camaraderie. After a couple of months Evan realized that only a few people were really doing the work. When he mentioned this to the group, kids simply told him he was uptight.

Because he was aware of our communal difficulties at Park Road, Evan didn't want to set himself up as an authority figure or to set himself apart from others at the house. But he became increasingly disturbed by the petty rebelliousness of the kids; the black anarchist flag hanging on the porch served primarily to alienate neighbors. Kids at the house were arrested at the Watergate demonstration following the Chicago Seven verdict as well as during the University of Maryland strike in the wake of the Kent State massacre. When they were arrested the second time, one kid was carrying drugs. Luckily the police didn't search anyone.

Evan felt the kids were acting in a foolishly provocative way, even though he shared their strong dislike for the police. (Their house was across the alley from a police station. Before each demonstration, beaded, mustached, Mod Squad types would emerge from the station house and move down to the demonstration site, where they would provoke violence and then help beat and arrest other demonstrators.) Evan began to feel that Madison Street's "revolutionary" posturing was mainly an excuse to rebel in other ways, to "get their rocks off." Fred returned from Berkeley spouting Weathermanese, talking of "pigs" and "trashing" without having gone through the serious conflicts that drove Weathermen to their conclusions. Instead, he displayed a disturbing revolutionary faddism.

Meanwhile three local kids began coming over regularly to smoke dope. One of the three had recently been arrested for possession of hard drugs. Evan liked the three guys but was worried that their presence would enhance Madison Street's image as the "hippie house." Jeff met a young black police cadet in the local doughnut shop who claimed Madison Street was under surveillance. Even then only Evan, Carol, and Phyllis felt the need to be "cool."

The conflict within the house erupted one night when Evan and Carol were cooking spaghetti. Since they only had a small pot, they decided to make two batches. The kids served themselves large portions the first time around, leaving none for Evan and Carol. Evan exploded at the kids. "They're spoiled and thoughtless," he said later. "They expect everything to be done for them."

Evan was bitter because the kids hadn't lived up to his expectations. Because they all worked together so well in the beginning, he assumed that their adolescent conflicts had been resolved. Yet they were still adolescents, supported by their parents, not yet forced by the necessity of survival to think beyond "today." The commune convinced Evan and Carol that they needed to live with older people.

In May they decided to abandon the house. The landlady had refused to make necessary repairs. They countered by refusing to pay rent. Further rumors of a bust had increased tension and paranoia. All of them were eager to leave. The group seemed somber about breaking up, yet relieved. I don't think any of them felt they had failed.

Madison Street did not become a stable community, but the kids there communicated; to communicate is not necessarily to agree. Perhaps kids need most to break away from their liberal compulsion to mediate all differences. Perhaps nothing could be healthier than to say "Fuck you" and "Fuck you too" out loud. Kids living in communes had the chance to tear down some of the walls, to throw away the phony cooperativeness that schools encourage. They could begin to relate as people.

Kids who lived at home could hardly understand the daily intensity that Madison Street took for granted.

For months I had been planning a trip, ostensibly to visit other schools in the Northeast. In mid-May six of us, four of whom lived at home, set out in our VW bus. I hoped the trip would give us a better perspective on our project.

After visiting schools in Philadelphia and New York we realized that these city schools lacked cohesiveness and direction— they were falling apart. As in our own school, physical dispersion prevented people from coming together spontaneously. Our next stop was the Colaberg school, forty miles outside of New York City. As we drove up and saw kids, loud and long-haired, hanging from the windows, we thought we had stumbled upon Lord of the Flies. We had brought city vibrations with us—we couldn't relate to the earthy, tree-swinging freedom with which the Colaberg kids taunted us. When they took us to a nearby waterfall we began to relax. We all took off our clothes and swam together. This was our first really intimate experience, and it made an indelible impression on us.

That night we camped out in the woods, seemingly light-years from New York City. Two of the Colaberg people came up and talked with us. They told us their school was in danger of closing, because the people who started it ten years ago were no longer open to new ideas. When the school began, it was quite a radical project. Now, they said, the school had gotten bogged down in the ego trips of the founders. I never discovered what the exact issues were in the Colaberg conflict, but I related what the two people said to my own experience in Washington. I realized that Joel and I, in our attempts to transmit the lessons we had learned the first year, had limited the experience of the new people in the school. That night I decided definitely to leave the school.

Our next stop was Cambridge, which, after Colaberg's idyllic rural setting, depressed us. We were eager to be off to the country once again. The next afternoon we left for the New Community School in New Hampshire, an hour's drive from Cambridge. We were greeted warmly there and were treated to a fine vegetarian dinner. We liked the place instantly.

Shortly after dinner two men came in, both drunk and obviously looking for a fight. I wasn't sure what their relationship was to the community. They were too old to be students and not the type who usually become free-school teachers. One of the drunks, Frank, who I later found out lived at the house, became angry at Alan, one of our people. Frank thought Alan was trying to take away his beer.

The actual issue didn't matter—there was violence in the air. The men then began to ask me ridiculous questions designed to provoke a fight. I asked them why they were being so aggressive. Just then someone else, who I assumed lived there (I later learned he was a visitor also), echoed my feelings. "You sure aren't making people feel at home," he said.

Frank leaped up and chased the kid around the room with a frying pan. One of the men in the house began talking calmly to Frank, absorbing his verbal artillery and coming close to taking physical blows too. I expected to become involved in the fray momentarily, and I uneasily grabbed a chair.

I wasn't too sure how to confront these guys. Their stupid cruelty struck an old chord in me. They revived the image of the toughs of my childhood whom I never made peace with. I could not demean myself to reason with them as this fellow was doing. I decided this community did not know how to deal with bullies. As long as their hands were extended in peace, the bullies would take advantage of them. The two men doted on being treated as special cases. They weren't about to trade power for love.

We decided to get into the bus and leave. I felt that the community had obviously experienced this before. If this was so I didn't want to be there. Mary expressed a strong disgust for them. With uncharacteristic hardness, she told us that if they came near her she would kill them. Her childhood, too, had been spent fending off lechers and bullies. Now she had revealed a part of herself that she rarely allowed to emerge. We were about to leave when one of the women from the commune came out to talk with us.

"I wish you wouldn't leave under these circumstances. All of us want you to stay," she said.

"Look," I answered, "this seems to be your own community problem. I can't relate to the way you appease this guy."

"It looks to me as if you're running away too. If we're all groovy people, then we should be helping each other."

"You can only solve the problem by coming to grips with it yourselves. There's no such thing as the Lone Ranger and Tonto, who swoop down and make everything right."

"Yeah, but how could you simply walk out and leave just one or two people to deal with those maniacs?"

"I didn't notice any of your other people restraining them. Everyone else disappeared. I figured that you must be used to it by now, that you have established a nice comfortable, sadomasochistic relationship. Otherwise these assholes wouldn't be tolerated."

"We are intimidated by Frank. We're afraid of him, but we also want to help him. Up till now we haven't felt strongly enough to expel him from the community. He's an Indian, he's had a fucked-up life, and people here sincerely want to relate to him. But it hasn't worked. Each time we extend ourselves or give him another chance he shits on us. I've had it. I want to have a community meeting right now to decide once and for all how we will handle this. I'd like you people to stay for the meeting."

I looked at everyone—we had decided to stay. At the meeting most of the people agreed that Frank and his friend were a menace to the community, but they were reluctant to expel him. They were afraid he would make trouble for them in town, close down the school, as he had frequently threatened. But finally they decided, if rather weakly, that they would ask him to leave when they saw him again. (He had gone for the evening.) More important, they would act as a group, so that no one person alone would have the burden of restraining him if the situation arose. They were profoundly afraid of this guy, and I realized that I was too.

The next day when he returned he was given "one more chance." The community had neither the strength to throw him out nor to effectively control his violent outbursts. They were unwilling to deal with the issue directly, partly because they felt guilty about the Indian thing. One of Frank's defenders said, "I feel we owe him something because we're white and he's an Indian who's been fucked-over."

"Bullshit!" I shouted. "I want to help him, but not because I feel guilty about it. There's no such thing as original sin. If my ancestors screwed the Indian—which they didn't—that doesn't make me an exploiter, especially if I'm doing my best to leave the exploiter class. Everyone of us here is struggling to change things, and I don't think we should be the object of his anger. But we're convenient scapegoats. It's much easier to fuck-over some hippies than the Bureau of Indian Affairs. They don't feel guilty but we do. That's why he does it to us—we let him do it. He can sense our guilt, that he can do anything to us and still be welcome."

Another person there approached the question from a different angle. "If you are going to the country to escape hassles or bad people, you're really deluding yourselves. Maybe you can eliminate Frank, kick him out. But how will you deal with it the next time? Because there are a lot of fucked-up people. You can't say a magic word and make them disappear. Sometimes you have to accept them—not let them do their thing because you feel guilty, but treat them like you do anyone else. When Frank does something wrong, tell him as if he were your own brother. If there is really feeling behind it, you can stop him."

I realized that if we were strong enough, we could "police" Frank in a nonviolent way. It would have taken strength and fearlessness to say "If you get violent here, you leave" and make Frank know we meant it. I'm not saying it's easy. I'm not sure I could have done it. But I realized that nonviolence is not the same as pretending violence doesn't exist.

Two days at the New Community left us exhausted. We realized how one-dimensional our day-school experiences had been, how useless classroom discussions were unless they occurred in a real context. As Matt said, classes were "ivory-tower bullshit." For the first time the commuters realized what was behind our "living-learning" rhetoric.

Our city communes did give "Philosophy" another dimension. Yet they could not overcome the alienation and isolation of the city. The farm work—the cow, the garden—at New Community gave their collective life a focus that is rare in a city commune. They had an ideal sort of privacy; when they needed to, they could come together on short notice. I thought of all the hours I had wasted driving people around the city.

We left New Community with a realistic enthusiasm about rural life, aware of the conflicts and difficulties involved, yet convinced that it was worth trying. Later in the summer Matt traveled to British Columbia with a group of friends to buy land, Anne moved to a farm in Vermont, and I returned to the New Community.

The intensity of living on the bus proved threatening to some of the people who hadn't lived communally in the past. As in our other communes, we underestimated the strain of being together twenty-four hours a day. Sometimes we used the place we were visiting to escape each other. When this was impossible, prolonged contact led to extraordinary tension. One night in Toronto we were returning from a Chinese restaurant. All of a sudden everyone in the bus was laughing and screaming hysterically at nothing, at everything. Pam and Mary, both usually quiet, were carrying on in uncharacteristic fashion. The scene reminded me of Randy Shaw's raucous excursions to the local ice cream parlor, our first commune's attempts to express the frustration of trying to communicate. Like the school communes, we hadn't become a cohesive community. Yet when we returned we felt a strong bond. We had shared something special. It seemed as if we'd been gone a long, long time.

Our two-week trip was a microcosm of the school. We were voyagers and voyeurs, turned on to new things, yet never really involved. The school was a journey of this sort, opening up people's senses, yet only letting them taste briefly. To experience more deeply, you had to get off the bus. Some got off at Madison Street, some at various art studios; I got off at a farm. Others just got on different buses. This is what we had set out to do—to let people re-sort their lives, to help them along the road, to help them find a road. I finally understood that our transience was a sign of our success.

CHAPTER V

Steve: Teaching and Adolescence

Indeed family, community and school combine—especially in the suburbs—to isolate and protect the youth from the adventure, risk and participation he needs. The same energies that relate him at this crucial point to nature result in a kind of exile from the social environment.

> Peter Marin, *The Open Truth and Fiery Vehemence of Youth*

When someone is seeking, it happens quite easily that he only sees the thing he is seeking; that he is unable to find anything, because he is only thinking of the goal he is seeking, because he has a goal, because he is obsessed with his goal. Seeking means to have a goal, but finding means: to be Free, to be receptive, to have no goal. You, a worthy one, are perhaps a seeker, for in striving toward your goal, you do not see many things that are under your nose.

> Hermann Hesse, *Siddhartha*

When young people who are otherwise very different from one another share skills, goals, and a common area of experience, each helps the others to understand their own uniquenesses, which greatly facilitates self-definition. The common skills and goals provide a reference point; the differences then add dimensions.

> Edgar Friedenberg, *The Vanishing Adolescent*

168

Starting the school was the radical act. But we carried it out in unoriginal ways.

Kathy

Decisions were ours to make, publicity was ours to write, money ours to raise. There was no one to blame. We could do what we wanted. We could create an educational community which would be open, flexible, contemporary, humane. Or so we supposed, since there was no external control.

The disintegrating effect of this kind of freedom is classic. You find that most of your thinking has been reactive, and that your powers for original decision are undeveloped. It is very difficult in this situation not to import the patterns of old rivalries, not to find them lingering like deposits in the soul. It is very difficult to abandon all one's former supports and to move forward in unfamiliar contacts. There are almost no handles in the situation except one's own bootstraps. When you can do what you want to do, what will you do?

M. C. Richards, *Centering*

When we first talked about starting a school we wanted the commune to be a place where we could break down barriers between teachers and students, between "adults" and "kids." In actuality the commune accentuated the cultural and emotional differences between the different age groups. We also hoped the commune would offer the kids a reprieve from the fierce and unfair demands of the middle-class American family. Yet we soon re-established some of the more destructive family roles within our own household.

Nevertheless, living together unleashed all of the energy thwarted by lesson plans and seating plans. The first two months were euphoric. They were the beginning of an intense learning experience; looking back on it, a few of the kids said it seemed like five or ten years. We fascinated each other—each of us was doing a different thing. Yet all of our activities intermeshed, complemented each other. More than ever, learning was action and interaction. When we sat around the dining-room table at Madison Street we felt the electricity of shared experience and activity: Charlie's poetry, Arthur's Go game, which intrigued everyone, Audrey sewing or cooking macaroni and cheese, Jeremiah and Val reading *Journey of Albion Moonlight* to each other, me taping rock and roll records late into the night. I remember Jeremiah sitting in our cramped kitchen and singing prophetically about Bob Dylan's dream.

All of us, young and old, were leaving an environment that had caused us daily pain and unhappiness. Each of us was experiencing the joy of release, of liberation from a system that had suppressed energies and feelings we now longed to express. And there were no apparent authoritarian figures—no parents, teachers, or administrators—in our school to repress us.

Our pioneering spirit created another strong bond between us. Charlie called the school "one of the first ships to be launched," "a frontier," an "exploration." Many people in the school felt that we were carrying on an experiment that had never been tried before. Few realized that our community had a kinship with many other utopian efforts in our history. Our feeling that what we were doing was unprecedented appealed to our sense of bravado.

More than anything else, we reinforced each other's enthusiastic visions. We rarely criticized each other. Unconsciously we must have felt our project was too fragile, our ideas too precious to be marred by any serious conflict. We submerged our differences because we wanted desperately to succeed at our own project.

In the excitement of our early months we viewed the authorities as the major threat to our existence. We expected the zoning board to close us down or the narcotics squad to stage a raid at any moment. These external threats welded us together and raised our morale at a time when unity was critical to our survival. But they also diverted our attention from solving the difficult problems of living together, from reconciling our diverse personalities and life styles.

During our early months the school cemented bonds between younger and older people, for in a sense we were all adolescents—in conflict with society, acting to break the economic and cultural bonds in which we had been raised, trying to define ourselves in a new way. Most of the older people felt a strong affinity for the youth culture because they had rejected so much of their adult identities. The older people attracted to this adventuresome project were themselves rootless and unstable, seekers who had rebelled against the straight life and who looked on the project as a new start.

Randy, for example, was a former seminarian who was at the end of his rope as a junior high school teacher. Richard, an old friend of mine who had joined the school in October, had recently graduated from college and had no idea what he wanted to do. Even Arthur, who appeared to be the most stable of the adults, had gone through many jobs and was now uncertain whether he could make it in his own project.

I envied the kids who were doing at sixteen what I could hardly do at twenty-two: they were making life decisions, acting the way they felt, loving. I viewed the youth culture as a spirit that I hoped would rejuvenate me. After a year as a gadfly in the school system I saw the school as a chance to build something positive, as my own rebirth.

All of us, at once, were trying to be "guides" and teachers, trying to prove ourselves, looking for an identity. Like myself, many of the older people sought nourishment from the kids, offering only weakness and confusion in return. When we first began living together our common confusion and isolation strengthened us. But as the school developed we began to behave like a dozen cripples fighting over a crutch.

We were so eager to get under way that we never fully discussed our ideas about education. Meetings and discussions bored us. They symbolized high school "committees," which never moved beyond the talking stage. Also, we reinforced each other when criticism would have been more appropriate. Our lack of consciousness about what we were doing made it easier for us to fall back into public school patterns.

Many of us, especially the older people, were concerned about "relating to the public schools." Before we left for our "island" we vowed to liberate the schools, because basically we felt guilty for leaving. We were smart enough to leave the stupidity of the school system. We were brave and spirited enough to try to make it on our own after being taught to fear insecurity. But we took on the extra burden of proving to the public schools that we could "educate" better than they could.

In talking with parents we sidestepped the real reason that kids left the public school—to create their own life styles. Instead, we assured them their kids would still be able to get into college from our school. We talked to them about classes, not the daily intimacy of living and working together. As we tried to convince people of the seriousness and value of our project we moved farther and farther away from our own ideals. We were freed of the burden of attending public school but were still attached, like exiles, to the words and values of school.

"We will all be teachers, we will all be students," our leaflet proclaimed. Yet some of us, dubbed "resource people," were quite obviously the teachers. At the initial meetings we, the resource people, presented ideas for courses, based on our own current interests or academic backgrounds. We expected the kids in turn to modify our plans and suggest new activities. But they were unprepared to do so. Public school and television had taught them to sit back and watch the show. Quite a few kids expected our school to be simply a higher grade of entertainment than public school.

The older people generally did not confront this passive attitude. Despite the rhetoric, we still thought of ourselves as teachers. All of us who "worked" full time at the school were given room and board in return. We had nothing to fall back on but our academic backgrounds—few of us possessed any other "marketable" skill. After a frustrating year in the classroom I looked forward to working with turned-on kids. I envisioned classes as absorbing yet informal seminars. All of us would be prepared to participate because we were interested and excited about the subject matter. There would be no need for me to prod.

At the same time I was aware of how manipulative teaching could be. Instead of giving my psychology class a definite orientation, I relied heavily on spontaneity, on the kids themselves. But my open-ended approach only added to their confusion. I didn't realize that since they only had a vague background in psychology they couldn't come up with their own program. We wavered for a long time, trying to decide whether to use a textbook for background or to just jump right into the middle of things.

Many kids were growing impatient with the ambiguous nature of the class. They hoped the school would provide more entertaining teachers, who, although noncoercive, would do the bulk of the work. I felt comfortable as a teacher-entertainer, and I knew I had a willing audience. Yet I wanted the kids to be instrumental in their own learning. And I needed to prove that it was the public school that had prevented me from doing a good job in the past.

After several weeks I hit upon *The Book,* by Alan Watts, as a way to excite the class. Unconsciously I had decided I was unwilling to do the necessary work to bring together a cognitive psychology course. Instead, I decided to start somewhere in the middle, to give kids a book that would turn them on. Although I wasn't lecturing or structuring the course, I was still perpetuating the passive public school style of learning. Rather than challenging the kids, I created a comfortable "happening" to ensure that we would have a good time and that no one would fail.

From there we moved on to Hermann Hesse—*Demian, Siddhartha,* and *Steppenwolf.* Then the class became more substantial. Hesse appeals to adolescents because his heroes are extraordinary, people of destiny. Kids don't identify with the empty antiheroes of Camus and Updike. They associate them with a dying society, because they run from the questions and wonder of life. By January we felt comfortable enough not to discuss *Siddhartha* when we realized we had nothing to say about it.

Because we were so afraid of failing, we spent a great deal of energy trying to make classes work. In their eagerness to try everything, kids rapidly overextended themselves. After a while some decided they preferred staying up all night at the commune to preparing for a course, or after reading a few pages of a book they realized they weren't interested after all. Others decided to work for only one course. Narrowing of interests is a perfectly natural process at a free school. Yet all of us felt guilty about fading classes. Unconsciously we incorporated the public schools' definition of learning. We still thought of classes as the only way to learn. Whenever parents asked about the school we listed all of the classes going on, even though we knew that there were more important things happening. It seemed as if we held classes so that we could justify our existence with some tangible activity.

Many of the older people were unaware of their academic prejudice. Most of us in our twenties had been to college and saw words and books as the key to learning. Younger people felt more comfortable with mixed media. They could read, listen to music, do any number of things at the same time. Not all of us were that versatile—thus the conflict over noise in our house.

Kids were much more creative and adventuresome in finding things to do. Sam and a couple of other kids spent a few weeks planning to capture a penguin from the zoo. After a while they abandoned their plans but in the process learned a good deal about penguins. Many kids used psychedelic drugs to heighten their awareness. When I finally took acid, the aspect of it that freaked me out most was the mixture of stimuli bombarding my defenseless consciousness. I liked to handle things one at a time, to always be in control. Kids were more open to the infinite existence. The term "getting kicks" really means a "kick in the ass" to the parents, a condemnation of their security hunger and future orientation.

Older people at the school often reinforced this parental role by hovering over kids, insisting they be "doing something." Yet few of us were involved in endeavors of our own. Kids realized how much we invested in classes and were reluctant to displease us by dropping out. Instead, they participated half-heartedly—they would do only half of the reading but would still come to class at the appointed time. Then the teacher would do most of the talking or the class would drift into a tangential discussion.

We feared failure because we had never learned to learn from our mistakes. "In public school," Kathy said, "you learn that you must never, never, never fail, because failure is a reflection of yourself. If you fail, you're bad, you've failed as a person." In the past we had been marked and judged by our mistakes. Now we were trying to prove we were not failures, but we only had public school criteria—classes—as a frame of reference. Classes were not particularly valuable in themselves, but we used them as a crutch to prove that we were actually doing something. We were evidently frustrated, yet no one dared to soundly criticize the classes. We continued to go through the motions, afraid of exposure like a bunch of naked emperors.

We also had a hard time confronting each other—a problem many communes have. We rarely were able to explode when it was most appropriate; we saved up our rage and expressed it on irrelevant occasions. Staughton Lynd remembers that his experience at Macedonia Community in Georgia taught him the importance of "direct speaking": "If you are going to the altar, or for that matter the cow shed, and you discover in your breast you have a difference with your brother, take him aside and go straighten the bloody thing out with him. Don't, above all, go to some third person and start gossiping." Somehow we associated making strong demands on people with being "authoritarian." We were still chained to our past, to our experiences in families and in public schools.

We responded reflexively to the violence we saw on the outside by trying to avoid conflict among ourselves. Within the commune, however, our conflicts surfaced quickly. Although I embraced the youth culture, liked rock music, and used drugs, I disliked the disorder in the house. I thought that a clean kitchen was important—most kids couldn't care less, or pretended not to care. I couldn't stand the McLuhanesque barrage of stimuli that pervaded the house. People tripping at the house made me uncomfortable and, in addition, kept me up all night.

Older people, partly because they were legally responsible for the commune, were more concerned with "responsibility" and "consequences." Kids had come from a school system where no real responsibility had been given them, where they took nothing seriously. To those who had had no contact with the law or jail, being busted was a remote possibility. But the older people who had been active in the movement had a legitimate fear that they might be busted or the school closed down. To some of the kids, Arthur and Joel must have seemed terribly paranoid. Youthful bravado prevailed on all of us to be groovy—to let strangers crash, to be casual about drugs, provocative about life styles. Afraid of appearing uncool, adults at the school tried to cover up any misgivings they might have had about activities the kids were involved in. When we were assertive we often acted like policemen, enforcing laws that we abhorred ourselves.

During our early months we did not realize how much our commune resembled the homes the kids had recently left—we preferred to believe that we were the avant-garde of a new life style, free from parental pressure. Yet our parents lived so strongly within us that simple tasks like dishwashing created incredible conflicts. "If I am free from my parents," the argument went, "then I don't have to do dishes. Nobody therefore can make me do them." Of course, just presenting the conflict in this way proves that the person is still not free from his parents.

Consciously or unconsciously, Arthur reinforced the "father" role that kids had come to resent. He felt that a person who did not help support the house or do the chores did not "love" the community. The American father, Jules Henry points out in *Culture Against Man,* compensates for the harshness and competition of working life by focusing all of his love energy on his children. The father wants to be a "pal" to his kids, to entertain them, to become involved in their affairs. But, in fact, he competes with his wife for the affection of their children. And the child comes to feel the pressure to love his parents *for what they can do for him* rather than for what they are. Instead of overtly punishing the child for his transgressions, parents invoke guilt and vaguely threaten loss of love.

Many of the people at the house felt that some of Arthur's solutions were correct. (Kathy, for example, thought that something should be done about the mess and wasn't hostile to the idea of a cooking or cleaning schedule.) Yet they balked at his solutions, because he so resembled a father trying to buy love with guilt. Meetings deteriorated into accusations and counteraccusations. "You don't care," said Arthur. "You are an authoritarian motherfucker," said the kids. We were not prepared for such a confrontation—the school had been such an idyllic place. Kathy felt that the disorder in the house was bad but that it was almost worth it to have all of the other good things going on. For others this was the first house in which they felt at home, where they could do as they pleased. Now the school threatened to take their freedom away, just as public schools had. Many kids were extremely sensitive to criticism—their concept of themselves was so fragile that any bit of criticism or shouting frightened them. An unwritten law of the house said you never confronted anyone with his bad habits for fear he might reveal yours. Silence was our defense.

Kids despised anger, not for the momentary outburst of honest emotion but for the pent-up emotion released at the same time. When parents had gotten angry at them it was often the culmination of tension from a frustrating day or a frustrating lifetime. Kids rightfully don't want to be blamed for what their parents do with their own lives. They view their parents' displaced anger as punishment for their being. Therefore kids associate anger and shouting and criticism with a judgment of their very existence.

Kids retaliate by denying any evil in themselves. At first our commune perceived outside authorities as the embodiment of evil. Yet we found "impurity" in our own household when we discovered we couldn't all get along with each other. I don't think it would be exaggerating to call the expulsion of Arthur, Ira, and Bill from the community a ritual, an exorcism of evil, a symbolic killing of the father. The ceremony began when Joel and Greg arrived wearing strange hats, mysteriously handing out beer, spreading "joy"—a ruse to deny the real conflict. When the conflict once again broke openly at the meeting, the "exorcisers" began hugging each other, to turn inward away from the evil. The lines had been clearly drawn. To accept their hug was to rejoin the fold, to once again become members of this strange culture that knew evil only as victims. To remain outside the circle was to admit unworthiness, impurity of soul and intentions. When Bill and Arthur hung back they were proved heretics. The "authoritarian motherfuckers" had been expelled.

Thus reassured, the rest of us went back to living together only to find the roots of our problems and "evil" in ourselves. We couldn't meet our own impossible standards of perfection —in spite of ourselves, we were often angry, selfish, foolish, spiteful, cruel. Maybe we created these criteria in response to the hypocrisy and greed of our elders. Perhaps we had internalized these criteria to deal with an insanely imperfect world. In Greg's words, "We were oppressed by our idea of utopia."

Like middle-class parents, older people at the school attached themselves to the kids in order to fill a need in their own lives. Jules Henry in *Culture Against Man* describes this phenomenon in the family:

> . . . the father is liked because he is the son's companion in the son's activities. Rarely does a child like his father because he is allowed to participate in the father's activities. This is extraordinary when viewed in the perspective of the culture of the world and even in the perspective of the not-too-distant rural past in America. There the son, and the daughter too, took pleasure in being permitted to take part in the parents' activities. In American culture, the demand is more often that the parents, especially the father, enter the child's world, not the other way around.

Rather than involve his youngsters in his work, which is often dull and petty, the American father becomes a part of the kids' world. He takes them on trips to the zoo or coaches their Little League team. He is no longer a person in his own right. Instead, he is valued as an entertainer, judged by how much he can give.

Most of the older people in the school related to kids in this way. We had few skills to offer—only a vague need to help, to teach a nebulous something. Unsure of our own skills and interests, we met kids on their own turf. We were so sure kids had the answers that we fully subjected ourselves to the youth culture.

Like fathers, we appeared to have no life of our own outside the family-school. To my older friends outside the school I was "Steve from the school," and when we got together, all we talked about was our project. But after all, the school was my "thing." I was skilled in doing organizational non-things like correspondence and setting up activities. But I couldn't teach tangible skills such as writing or music. Like the father, I saw this "family" as a refuge from the competitive world and sought to get more out of it than I put in.

As in the family, older people competed consciously, and sometimes unconsciously, for the kids' attention and approval. None of us wished to appear authoritarian or uptight. Despite the filthiness of the house, I tried to avoid confrontation with the kids. Even Arthur was reluctant to play the traditional father role, fearing he would be unloved if he did. Evan spoke bitterly about "spoiled kids," yet he tried to be one of them, ignoring all but the most blatant transgressions. Having little or no culture of our own, we feared banishment from the youth culture.

Our fear of being "authoritarian" sometimes became a form of irresponsibility. When a girl in the school needed an abortion and Joel became really concerned about it, Randy shrugged it off. He advised Joel not to get uptight about it, that "it would all work out." It did work out, but only after Joel had spent a great deal of energy trying to find someone to help the girl.

Not only did we resemble the family socially but we re-established the same kinds of economic relationships. Even while living at the commune, most kids continued to be supported by their parents. The community supported those whose parents balked at paying for room and board. It was only fair—why should a kid be penalized because his parents didn't like the school?

We didn't make demands on either those supported by their parents or those supported by the school (that is, supported by

other people's parents). Talk of student-organized fund-
raising projects made no sense in the context of our warm-
mother-community whose "tit" was always available. Kids resented our belated attempts to change this relationship, our
demand that they "bring money into the community"—just as
a kid resents being told to "go out and get a job" after being
supported by his parents for sixteen years. The fact that the
older people, too, were living on the parents' tuition money
made it difficult to talk about creating a self-sufficient community. The kids naturally felt that Arthur was self-righteous
when he suggested that kids get a job while he himself was
being supported by the school.

In our meetings we were always talking about "plans" for
raising money—having rock benefits, making and selling
candles, jewelry, leather goods—but these projects only
infrequently got off the ground. People were initially very enthusiastic but then quickly lost interest. We never pushed each
other hard enough to make our "plans" a reality. This is a
weakness that people in many radical projects have. Staughton
Lynd describes how people working for SNCC tried to pin
each other down at meetings:

> "It's very nice, the opinion you just expressed, but I'm not
> sure I heard you say that you were the person planning to do it."

> "Yes, it would be very good to have a voter registration project
> in Macomb, but when are you leaving?"

All of us in the commune took on distinct parent or child
roles. The "parents" took "responsibility" for their "children," did most of the work, and resented the "ingratitude" of
the kids who didn't work. More than once Arthur recommended that Charlie get a job in a tone not unlike my
mother's when I was sixteen and unemployed for the summer.
After I began to do things around the house I discovered I had
incorporated quite a bit of my mother into my personality. I
tended to be a martyr and to come down on anyone who did
not readily appreciate my sacrifices. When I left on the trip in

February I was really saying, "Wait until I leave. Then they'll see how much they need me."

Meanwhile kids retaliated by acting irresponsibly. After Randy and a few others came from Baltimore with the case of vinegar and a case of hamburger relish, I hit the ceiling. "Well," they told me with great indignation, "if you don't like the way we do things, why don't you do them yourself?"

We had been so involved in actually getting the school off the ground, so absorbed in our own excitement, that we never talked about what it meant for kids to leave their parents. None of us examined carefully the school's dependence on parents, nor did we consider that kids might be unwilling to give up the comforts of home. Most of us assumed that our divergence from adult society meant that we could accept support from parents without being tainted by their values. We would use them, "rip them off," as the fashionable rhetoric goes. But we failed to see that dependency is a double-edged sword.

Tuition money and our grant made it unnecessary to find funds on our own. When our funds ran out we weren't strong enough to raise money and maintain a community at the same time. Within the commune, kids expected "freedom" to do as they pleased, yet they needed parents in the form of nursemaids who would cook and wash their clothes. They mistakenly expected these surrogate parents not to make the same demands on them that real parents did. Family relationships continued because kids refused to let go of the comfort of the family. Likewise, our project could not give up the material comforts of our society. We were tied to the purse strings as well as the apron strings.

This is the irony of the middle-class youth revolution. How many young rural communitarians living very close to the earth make visits to their parents in Scarsdale? How many campus activists discuss tactics at poolside while father rides the hills in his power mower? How many kids speak of Poverty and Imperialism as they sit down to a voluptuous Friday-night dinner? I am not judging these people—I am only pointing out how much there is to lose and how hard it is to let go. Some radicals, like the Weathermen, identify with the oppressed, as if to repent for their money and "skin privilege." But guilt and denial are both bad bases for a movement.

The school was too flimsy a basis for a commune. We didn't rely on each other for either financial or emotional survival. Parents and the foundation gave us food, money, drugs, music, and the city provided entertainment. After the first few months we no longer excited each other. Few of us brought anything new into the commune, or did any work on the outside the first year. The rest of us simply exhausted and ravished each other. We lacked nourishment from the outside.

When Greg returned with a completed piece of work we were excited. Because Greg was living with us, we felt in some way connected with his creation. Not that we took credit for it—we just felt as if we had grown. Art work in the commune we took for granted. But Greg's work, done in a metal shop in far-off southeast Washington, symbolized our need for reinforcement and contact from the outside. Whenever anyone returned from a trip he raised our spirits with tales of this place or that. Other kids became excited, not only by the stories but by visible changes in the traveler. Everyone needed to travel for a while. But too often we settled for vicarious pleasure, like a housewife tied to her chores listening to some traveling salesman.

The school, when conceived, was a means—a means to break out of society's mold, to get a sense of self, a means to adventure. Just the act of starting the school was an adventure: many of us who handed out leaflets did so at the risk of arrest; others left warm and comfortable homes to move into a house we still hadn't found. The first step, leaving public school, made subsequent steps easier. Once out of school, kids began to examine and fondle the real world—they hopped freights, picked fruit out west, traveled to the Chicago convention, camped out with the Poor People at Resurrection City. Mobility became the key: emotion was translated into motion. "I think best at sixty miles an hour," one kid summed it up.

The commune absorbed much of this furious energy in the early months as long as kids were mainly concerned with getting to know each other—tripping, staying up late, eating, and talking together. We moved among one another, sharing past and present adventures, gloried in new-found truth. But the older people in the commune were unprepared to confront the transience and wanderlust of youth. The older people "settled down" more quickly and expected the younger to follow suit. Despite our rhetoric about "exploding the classroom," we still viewed ourselves as teachers, or at least as nondirected supervisors.

Like the modern American family, our existence became "apartmentalized." Rather than using the resources of the city, we clung together in little households. Instead of welcoming visitors, we drew sharp distinctions between "people in the school" and "outsiders." Only a few traveled to any extent. The rest stayed home, no doubt feeling "responsibility to the house."

We began as a refuge from parental expectations. Now we imposed unreasonable demands of our own. We, the older people, were the parents who sacrificed to give kids the support we had never had. How could they be so ungrateful as to want to leave? We imposed the same kind of feelings as the overprotective mother. Our house had become a frightful parody of the American family.

We tried to short-circuit the intensity of adolescence and transform it into a project of our own design. A few of the kids "outgrew" the school because we couldn't change as quickly as they could. Jeremiah felt the school was a "smaller world," an environment constructed for kids—"smaller than his potential," to use Peter Marin's words. He wanted to participate in the outer world of risk and adventure. Like public school teachers, we shielded ourselves from intense experiences, from strange people—like Mad John—who might distract us from the smaller world we had set up.

Like Siddhartha's friend, our vision was limited by our goals. In our attempt to become an institution we overlooked the real value of the school—to free kids from the confines of public school, to give them a place of their own, a place where they could have time to sort out the commitments they wanted to make. Our school fulfilled this need for many kids. As a result they were less apt to criticize the school's shortcomings, which were apparent to us. The chance to leave public school was liberation enough. "The free school was just the opposite of public school," Kathy said. "Here people actually had control over their own lives. They could make up the rules or get rid of them, they could really get a grasp on what was happening, they were people who really wanted to learn."

The purpose of a free school is not to be coherent. Its most valuable function is to allow kids, in Edgar Friedenberg's words, "to respond specifically to each other." We realized that such classes as dance, art, and creative writing were particularly successful because they met the immediate needs of a person leaving a manipulative and competitive system—the needs for creativity and communication. Kids needed to break out of the passive television-consumer mentality and assert themselves as skilled individuals, neither expendable nor interchangeable. They needed to share their skills and experiences with others; part of the discovery of self is sharing one's discoveries. Public schools are so massive and depressing that kids rarely have a chance to communicate with each other. When we ran our summer program we discovered that kids who came from the same schools and had similar interests often didn't know each other.

Essentially, public schools pervert the creative energy they arouse, isolate it, make it competitive, and turn it into a commodity. The most important thing kids learn about creative work in school is to put it away when the bell rings. Because "art," after all, is meant to be a diversion, a hobby. Art is something you can take out and put away. Instant art—you buy it in the supermarket. When a bored housewife consults a psychiatrist she is told to "take up ceramics." Real creative energy, Theodore Roszak points out in *Making of a Counter-Culture,* is like that of the tribal shaman, whose magic defined and consumed his entire life: "magic not as a repertory of clever stunts, but as a form of experience, as a way of addressing the world." Western society "addresses the world" in a manipulative rather than a descriptive way.

School creative arts emphasize competition rather than communication. From the time the kindergarten teacher hangs up the "best" paintings to the "What is a good citizen?" essay contest, one ego is pitted against the other, one set of experiences is judged better than another. Later on in life people read "best sellers" and use their artistic knowledge for cultural one-upmanship rather than for self-knowledge.

In public school, creative activity is almost always reserved for superior students. The exception is shop courses, which, of course, tend to be the most authoritarian in tone. Possibly, bright kids get more leeway because they are articulate enough to ask for it. More likely, school officials are convinced that kids who do poorly on intelligence tests have nothing to say anyway. Those who can't paint or write or make their own clothes can still appreciate (that is, buy). I recall hearing a commercial on a slick "progressive" rock radio station in New York that begins with a soft guitar and a poetry reading. "We all can't write poetry, but we can express ourselves in what we wear. At Barney's Men's Shops . . ."

Once removed from the alienated high schools and affluent homes, kids at the school tended to consume less and create more. They became aware of the media's perversion of the "youth culture." Spontaneously, almost unconsciously, they began to create a culture of their own—not to overthrow American culture, just to fill the void. Their "youth culture" was a reaction against the depersonalization of technology. Unlike previous revolutionary movements, theirs is more social than economic. Most of the kids in the school had experienced affluence and were now searching for an alternative to it. They had seen the "best" of what American society had to offer and had rejected it.

Even the more "political" members of our community had rejected the struggle and martyrdom of the professional revolutionary. The revolution, they felt, was beginning now, with the way we lived, the way we related to each other. Individuals, not ideologies, were important. You shared your home, your dope, your belongings because it was "good Karma." Those who passed beyond parental support believed in a frontier-style self-reliance but at the same time rejected "hip" capitalism. When Simon began making leather vests he looked for a store that would sell them cheaply, so that they wouldn't be available only to rich hippies. Most of the kids couldn't conceive of music being private property—they boycotted the Woodstock movie because they resented exploitation of "their" music.

Although dope often has a passive, numbing effect on kids, it is at least an adventure, one of the few available in the Secure Society. In Peter Marin's words:

> . . . adolescents provide for themselves what we deny them: a confrontation with some kind of power within an unfamiliar landscape involving sensation and risk. It is there, I suppose, that they hope to find through their adventures the ground of reality, the resonance of life we deny them, as if they might come upon their golden city and return still inside it. . . . Theirs is a world totally alien to the one we discuss in schools; it is dramatic, it enchants them; its existence forms a strange brotherhood among them and they cling to it as though they had been to a fierce land and back. It is that which draws them together and makes of them a loose tribe. It is, after all, some shared experience, some kind of foray into the risky dark; it is the best they can do (*The Open Truth and The Fiery Vehemence of Youth*).

Sam also said something like this: "Drugs provide an orgiastic experience as referred to by Erich Fromm in the *Art of Loving*, whereupon the experience is repeated again and again for needs comparable to sex, sensationalism and beauty—on and on."

Curiously, drugs have also served as a basis for religion, which the Christians have long since abandoned in favor of science. All of the other seemingly "irrational" trips—Tarot cards, astrology, Buddhist chanting, macrobiotics—serve an important need for mysticism. They offer evidence of a world beyond Univac. Kids have canonized Ginsberg, Leary, and Hendrix to counteract the priesthood of Wernher von Braun.

Arthur, who had a background in science, picked up these vibrations—for the first few months science became observation and nature appreciation. Seeing the sunrise, watching the clouds, studying the river, are necessary steps to rid us of the illusion that "man is master of his environment." More recently, the furor over ecology has prompted interest in science. In our case it was a false start—few of us were willing to wade through technology to understand ecological problems in more than superficial terms. Yet some kids, after they get some perspective on themselves, will study science more deeply, if only to make humanistic sense of it. If they do decide to become scientists they will bring with them a sense of awe, something missing in today's facile technocrats.

Even before the school started I understood implicitly the need for adolescents to communicate with each other. I thought that a planned activity, like a sensitivity group, would break down the barriers more quickly. I had been exposed to this type of activity earlier in the summer and was eager to use it in our own community. We spent quite a few fall days in Rock Creek Park learning how to relax with each other, learning to touch and hold each other. During the first months this group activity reinforced the closeness we all felt. But the group ultimately lacked spontaneity and context. Rather than utilizing the real interpersonal situations that confronted us, we did "exercises." I had had neither the intuition nor the confidence to suggest the right exercise at the right time. Our group had little sense of continuity.

Had we run the sensitivity group in the commune for the commune people, we might have had the context we lacked. But we scarcely needed an encounter group in the commune. Communal issues were nearly always intense and personal. Daily living provided enough of an encounter. Although the commune may not have developed to fit our idea of "community," we succeeded in setting up an environment where kids could begin to live their own lives. As the kids emerged from dependency they learned some of the survival skills they had taken for granted while living at home: cooking, food buying, house maintenance, and finances. When Dave took charge of the bookkeeping for a few months the first year, his attitudes changed drastically. Now that money was more tangible to him, he became concerned with how it was spent. Those who began cooking out of necessity appreciated it more when others cooked. By the end of the first year kids were saying the same thing about sharing work as Arthur had said in November. The difference was that they had learned it by themselves, as a community. Slowly and painfully we had emerged from our closely guarded "privacy" to a realization of self-interest that included other people.

The commune provided reinforcement for what we were— we no longer saw ourselves as "freaks." As we came to trust each other we learned to accept ourselves, and we learned to accept change in ourselves. As Charlie said, "The commune burned out of us things which were redundant to other people."

Before she came to our school Kathy suffered severe headaches because of academic pressure. At our school she was free of impossible demands: "Not only did I get a chance to write, but I got a chance to read other people's work. Bob, for example, wasn't a professional writer, wasn't even a grown-up, yet he could write really well. I felt relaxed in the class—I didn't feel I had to write something perfect."

Kathy wasn't rejecting competence—just the competition that goes with it. The school helped kids become more competent. It was a unique consciousness-raising experience. Again Kathy: "I got a real shock when I went to the Woodstock festival last summer. There were thousands and thousands of kids here who seemed 'hip.' But when I talked with them they seemed so young and so confused: 'What's a commune? Free school—I don't know about that—will it work?' I was shocked that there were so many kids who hadn't even begun."

When kids left to do other things they took with them the strength to confront a stupid, impersonal system, a strength that comes from being on your own. After a year away from the school Kathy wrote:

> This past year I have been going to school in England at a somewhat inefficient private school. The teachers were really administrators who constantly hassled us with petty little rules. I felt older than most of the people at my new school. I found it easier

to verbalize than before. The school in Washington gave me such a secure basis—I couldn't have gone to that school in London without having spent the year at the free school. This year, I couldn't have written without having built up the sense of security at the commune and the school. For the first time many of us were on our own—I felt for the first time able to learn things by myself. In this sense, our school was an amazing success.

After the first year I, too, felt the school had helped me become stronger. I was confident that I was moving in the right direction now that I was part of a community that had built something together. Yet I couldn't appreciate the full impact of the communal experience. At the time I felt the intensity of the commune often interfered with learning. I looked forward to a less hectic, better-organized project the next year. But the second-year experience proved redundant to me. Since most of the new people were leaving the school system for the first time, I became much more of a "teacher-organizer" than I had been the first year. I spent so much time setting up activities for the kids that I largely ignored my own needs.

Throughout the second year I felt vaguely disturbed by the more formal role I had taken on. An incident toward the end of the year helped me understand how I related to the school. A local psychoanalyst, Rodolfo, had been conducting a class on dream interpretation which several of us attended regularly. Christine and Cynthia, two girls living at Irving Street, occasionally came to the class. When they did come they took part actively. But several times we waited fifteen or twenty minutes to start the class before we realized they weren't going to show up. Their casual attitude disturbed Rodolfo. He wanted to know definitely whether they intended to be in the class. If they did, he wanted them to attend regularly or not at all.

I only partly agreed with him. I felt the girls ought to notify us beforehand if they weren't coming to class. "Making the phone call," I said, "is a question of consideration for other people. It's a reasonable social demand. It's also reasonable for us to begin on time whether or not they have arrived. But whether they spend their time in the class in the first place—

that's their personal decision to make without pressure. Schools and parents have made too many confusing demands on them in the past. Now they are trying to decide which commitments they want to make. I find something really serious in their capriciousness, a test to find out if we really trust them. They don't know yet if they want to come on a permanent basis—an ultimatum might discourage them completely from becoming involved."

"But we haven't made any demands on them at all," Rodolfo insisted. "They've had enough time to decide whether they want to become part of this group or not. I feel justified in asking them once and for all. We aren't denying them a choice—we are just clarifying the choice and pushing them toward it. I'm serious about doing this class. Unless they are serious, unless they know why they're coming, unless they've actually chosen to come, I feel that we are wasting our time."

I was still unconvinced. Both girls seemed especially spoiled and flighty, yet I wasn't sure demanding full commitment wouldn't alienate them further. At the same time I realized Rodolfo could make clearer demands on students because he was so deeply interested in what he was teaching and was sure of what he had to offer. Even though my life revolved around the school more than his did, I did not feel as confident about my skills or the value of my subject matter. Rodolfo felt, I'm sure, that kids needed him more than he needed to be working with them.

I began to notice that the most fruitful relationships between kids and adults at the school occurred in our apprenticeship situations, where adults were doing something besides teaching and had a concrete skill or craft they could share with students. These people displayed a craftsmanship and self-discipline in their own work that made it easier for them to set high standards for the kids. Many kids had never seen adults so passionately involved in their work. Nevertheless, only two students worked as apprentices for any length of time—Greg and Joanne. Probably they were the only ones ready to focus their time and energy so heavily. Still, these adults served as models for everyone, as competent older people who had a tangible skill to share, who had made sense of their lives and maintained some degree of integrity in technological society. I realized I had related to kids not as a competent adult but as a fellow adolescent. This was not what I wanted and not what they needed.

In *Lives of Children,* George Dennison speaks of the "natural authority" of adults: "[Natural authority] is a far cry from authority that is merely arbitrary. Its attributes are obvious: adults are larger, are experienced, possess more words, have entered into prior agreements among themselves. When all of this takes on a positive instead of merely a negative character, the children see the adults as sources of certitude, approval, novelty, skills."

In public schools teachers rely more on arbitrary authority— textbooks, Board of Education directives—than on their authority as people. Our school gave adults more of an opportunity to break out of roles, to speak and act like themselves. As a teacher in a free school, however, I was trapped in a different sort of role. People expected me to provide entertainment and approval, to criticize only rarely, to say "do your own thing." Because I needed the school for my identity, most often I accepted the role. My uneven attempts to become authentic were a source of confusion and frustration for everyone involved. I acted like a combination Catskills social director and Mary Worth, at times thinking up "happenings" for kids, at other times hovering over their lives like a nosy old lady.

The vagueness I felt about my role at the school was due as much to a vacuum in myself as to a conflict over educational ideas. "Those who can, do. Those who can't, teach," said George Bernard Shaw; four years of liberal-arts education trained me to be a teacher in this sense. I picked up no satisfying skill, nothing that gave me a sense of accomplishment. Leaving the school system to work at the free school helped me understand how archaic and one-dimensional academics are. Still, I thought of myself primarily as a teacher. I felt lost without students, lost without a subject matter. At the beginning of the second year I was eager to do a class in American culture, but I soon realized how superficial the class was. We had some

good discussions, but the group had no focus, no common interest or problems, no direction. No one in the group was as
interested in the course as I was. And reluctantly I realized I
was no longer interested either. I felt restless, eager to follow
my new interests—music, writing, yoga, building. As I became
aware of myself outside a teaching relationship I knew that the
time had come to leave the school and become a learner again.

At the same time I had become disappointed in the "adult
commune" I was living in. In January, after the kids left
Jefferson Avenue, several older people moved in: Greg, a student at the school the first year whom I considered an older
person; Susie, a former Labor Department employee who
hoped to start a child-care center in Takoma Park; Joan, a free-
lance writer recently returned from three years' study at Cambridge; Ed, a Vietnam veteran working as a draftsman. For the
first month we were a happy, cohesive group, free of the parent-
child turmoil of the previous year. Mealtimes and evenings were
exciting—we enjoyed being together and learning about each
other. But all of us were away during the day: Susie and Joan
became involved with Women's Liberation and spent most of
their time with friends downtown, Greg was attending college,
Ed was working, Joel taught at a junior college, I spent my
time with school activities. Our commune fell apart because we
shared no important activity. There wasn't enough in the city-
suburban orbit to hold us together.

Our school trip to Canada and New England further convinced me that the city was stunting my growth. All of us returned to Washington feeling that any community within the
city was doomed to fail because there was so little in the city
worth preserving or defending. Matt Clarke expressed our feelings afterward when he said:

> This year's experiences have crystallized my feeling about working
> and about the city. Working teaches the value of money, mainly
> the shit you have to go through to get it to live. But I don't want
> to go out and get clerk jobs or work for the census bureau. In-
> stead, I want to find a place in the country where at least the
> hassles will be within yourself and of a dimension that you can

blindly to the consumer whistle. As he has become dependent on technology he has become farther removed from real life processes; he no longer understands how he relates to the world. His ignorance can be seen in the daily ingestion of food. He buys a frozen something at the supermarket—no idea where it comes from. He eats it, and shits in a clean, enameled rest room. Woosh! Down the toilet to God knows where, gone and forgotten, beforeless and afterless. Like his waste, his existence has no context. He floats along with no reference point except Astroturf and Ultra-Brite toothpaste. Western society is well on its way to eliminating pimples, yet its prolific excrement and pastel toilet paper threaten rivers and oceans.

Even as a radical in the city I was part of the effluent society. Although I was seeking new ways of relating, still I remained passive and uncreative. Saturday nights I restlessly searched the newspapers for movies to see. I used drugs and listened to music primarily as an escape. Headphones symbolize the city "head." His senses are plugged in, on a closed circuit. To avoid the city noise he must have his own "Muzak." He fills all gaps in his consciousness with stimuli, all hours with entertainment. He learns to clutter his time and space with "things" to avoid a confrontation with infinity, the world beyond the man-made.

At the farm I've been able to hear my own music and the sounds of living things around me. Looking at the sky puts the trivial into perspective. I sit on the hill and watch the hawk overhead and realize that primitive man probably understands the hawk better than I ever will. I've walked up the hill and felt joyously rooted. This is the first home I have ever had; I don't feel as if I own it, nor do I feel that I will be here forever. But I am an active part of things here. I milk the cow and I drink. I plant and pick vegetables and I eat. We feed our garbage back to the earth in a digestible form. I find nothing mysterious or alienated in my daily chores. All of them have a visible product. My work is related to basic rather than manufactured needs. I feel a new respect for physical work now that it's work for myself and at my own pace.

As I let my city "sophistication" crumble, I've learned some

handle. The trip helped me to see what the city did to people—
like those people in Philadelphia who tried high school organizing in the city and failed. In the city, you are always fighting
your environment—crime, drugs, police, other people cramped
together—and you are fighting the government. Perhaps going to
the country is really running away, but perhaps the problems of
the city are insoluble. But without a doubt, the city is offensive
to the senses and destructive to the spirit.

Those of us hoping to build an alternative to the competitive consumer life style found the city a difficult place to begin.
You cannot remain in the city without being tainted with its
coldness, its paranoia, its violence. To "survive," hippies buy
guns and sell bad drugs, blacks rob other poor people. I did
not wish to survive in this way. I didn't want to shoot people
who were trying to rob me, nor did I want to holler at kids
who were disturbing me with noise when they had nowhere
else to go. I had no desire to take out my frustrations on store
windows.

The city forces you into situations that trap your energy and
dehumanize you. People in the city live so close together that
they spend their time fighting each other instead of confronting the real causes of their problems. Even though we, too,
were outlaws, we came to realize the sirens did not toll for us.
Because we were white, the police afforded us some protection
against violence. When the same cop we despised for his prejudice and stupidity became a welcome sight, I knew that I had
to leave the city.

Initially I moved to a farm as a place to write and work for
the summer. After a month I found it impossible to return to
the city. Early in the fall I received a postcard from a friend
that implied I was "escaping reality" by living in the country.
But it's city life that is surreal and schizoid. Urban man spends
most of his energy shutting out unpleasant stimuli: the bad
air, the noise, the other desperate people. He believes that we
know more than people of any other age, that twentieth-
century life is better than life has ever been. Yet his life is out of
his control. He works at a job of dubious value and responds

remarkable things. Last fall I helped deliver a baby. I was excited and scared, but the situation was so natural that I automatically relaxed. Shortly after, I killed my first chicken. Chickens are not made in Colonel Sanders' factories to fit inside plastic bags. They are living things that squawk when they are killed. Slaughtering my own meat has not made me a vegetarian, but it has made me more conscious of what I put inside my stomach.

Not only does the farm provide a chance to relate to the physical environment but it facilitates relationships with other people. For this reason it is an ideal school. Since the fall we have had several younger people living with us, ranging in age from fifteen to twenty-one. We have experienced little of the noise and static that characterized the Washington school and have, in general, refrained from the parent and child roles that tore apart our city communes. The farm work that must be done is a focus for our activity. At the same time we have the time and space to be alone. Academic studies are in proper perspective—books move through the community, discussions arise spontaneously. Because we work and live together we communicate easily about our interests. There is really no need for classes. Most important, the life style itself, not particularly the adults involved, demands a commitment and discipline. It is as if the older people are sharing a valid way of living with the kids.

The farm is not totally dependent on the kids, although they play a large role in running it. Usually an older person, or one who has been here a while, initiates a project: milking the cow, caring for the chickens, feeding the goats, digging a garden. Gradually the jobs are taken over by the less experienced people. As they become more proficient they train someone else.

Our life style gives us privacy, yet puts us in touch with things outside of ourselves. We are not returning to the primitive. We are just offering a way to examine our roots, to see our relationship to the earth. Slowly we are understanding technology, using machines or discarding them on the basis of environmental needs as well as our own. We are learning to be symbiotic again, to give back some of what we take, to respect life and death.

This is my sane asylum. I'm learning to be responsible for myself, to act constructively. I'm not simply doing an internship to become a better revolutionary. I am living the revolution.

CHAPTER VI

Joel: Personal and Political Change

When we began organizing our project we saw it as an extension of our struggles to change the public schools. I had worked with activist students at Montgomery Blair to challenge the policies of the administration. We were constantly looking for the perfect organizing issue—detention halls, grading, the draft, the tracking system—the one that would spark the enthusiasm of the most students. But we became frustrated, because the administration had the power to parry any blows we could strike against it.

It used flexible tactics to manage whatever conflicts were raging in the school. It was willing to make small concessions— a liberal dress code, more independent study, a relatively free school paper—but would not grant students any effective control over curriculum, rules, the formulation of school policy. It was hard to fight people who could employ the rhetoric of educational reform so skillfully.

To make things even harder, most students in the school felt too impotent to act. They felt the risks were too great and the gains too meager to be worth the battle. Social life—driving around in a new car, going to the football game, getting drunk with the boys, going to Hot Shoppes to see "what was happening"—absorbed energies that might have gone into protest.

We paid a price for the work we did. The administration told Jeremiah that he could not come on school property and threatened him with arrest if he did. The principal and other teachers were always asking me to defend my activities; many of them just avoided me. They made me a scapegoat, projected anger they felt for their disaffected students. Everything would have been placid that year, they seemed to be saying, if I had never come to teach there. During the spring, at the height of our organizing for the free school, I was terribly apprehensive that I would be fired. The daily madness of Blair was burning me out; I was feeling less and less effective as an organizer. I came home from school exhausted and escaped my problems by going to sleep.

The idea for the school was born out of the frustrations that Jeremiah and many of the others felt. We were tired of suffering daily defeat and humiliation at the hands of the administration. We wanted to create our own school, to define ourselves as whole human beings—to cease acting like malcontents who had to rebel just to survive. But we felt guilty about abandoning our work, about leaving other students behind to pick up the pieces.

These feelings informed our early rhetoric about the goals of the free school. We argued that the project was one way of changing the character of the public schools. Our first leaflet said: "Visible alternatives to the present educational system should be available to the citizens of a community. Many of us find it impossible to imagine any other form of education than the daily drudgery we are subjected to. The establishment of the school can help the community to begin the task of educational reform." I wondered, though, whether our alternative would have any substantial impact on the Montgomery County system. Perhaps we were the perfect safety valve for a system in trouble. The project might drain off potential troublemakers and make life that much easier for the administration.

I had thought a lot about the fate of progressive schools in America. The mainstream institutions had largely ignored them. How much had Antioch affected the University of Ohio?

Or Goddard the University of Vermont? I was determined that we should not create another progressive school, an enclave for those privileged enough to afford it. But how were we going to prevent the same thing from happening to us? Maybe our school would become another cocoon the young could escape into, another trivial experiment. When we were planning the project we talked about having evening and weekend activities in our house for public high school students. We wanted kids to become involved in work projects, in apprenticeships, with institutions in the city. It would be great, we felt, if they could create their own project—a preschool, for example. But these were vague hopes, not at all the ingredients of a concrete program.

When the school started in the fall it was easy to forget the political vision that had inspired our first efforts. Building and sustaining a commune, struggling to live together, were much more immediate and urgent tasks. When I argued many times that we should spend more time talking to public school teachers and students about our experiences, I convinced very few people. Our community was too insular, I felt—we had withdrawn into our own heads.

But many of the kids in the school had never lived away from their parents before, let alone with students their own age. They found it exhilarating to have the time for self-exploration, to do nothing if they wanted to. I can only echo what Peter Marin said about his experiences at Pacific High School: "What we found was that our students seemed to need, most of all, relief from their own 'childhood'— what was expected of them. Some of them needed merely to rest, to withdraw from the strange grid of adult expectation and demand for lengthy periods of introspection in which they appeared to grow mysteriously almost like plants."

Because of my movement experience I felt that we should stimulate young teachers and students to organize their own schools and to make radical demands on their own administrations. The work that seemed most compelling to me—making our school into a force for political change—seemed artificial to the kids. I was asking them to support people trapped in public schools when they wanted first to liberate themselves. But understanding their needs didn't make things any easier for me. I was still impatient.

Many movement people have grown weary and frustrated because it takes white middle-class kids so long to acquire political consciousness. The interests and priorities of the organizers of "liberation schools" have often clashed with those of the students in them. Eric Mann recalls that many of the students in the Columbia Liberation School—organized the summer after the college strike—enjoyed folk dancing more than they did courses in Marxist economic theory.

A number of kids in a summer school organized by SDS in Takoma Park, Maryland (begun the summer of 1968), felt that the radicals were manipulating them. They resented the cadre's attempts to teach them the correct line, to recruit cannon fodder for the cause. High school kids often complain that movement people, like their teachers, fail to reveal their hidden agendas—that they mask their bias under a façade of objectivity.

The experience of some SDS people who worked in free schools was so frustrating that they started looking for more militant forms of action. Since free schools had made such a small dent on the society, they concluded that these projects were no longer a useful instrument of structural change. Bill Ayres, Diana Oughton, and Terry Robbins, who taught in the Children's Community, an elementary school in Ann Arbor, Michigan, all became Weathermen. The city inspectors hounded their school to death.

Counterinstitutions, their radical critics argue, are reformist —they divert people from the urgent struggle to change the "system." Carl Davidson's cogent analysis of the free university movement is a good example of this position:

> At best, they had no effect. But it is more likely that they had the effect of strengthening the existing system. How? First of all, the best of our people left the campus, enabling the existing university to function more smoothly, since the "troublemakers" were gone. Secondly, they gave liberal administrators the rhetoric, the analysis and sometimes the manpower to coopt their programs

and establish elitist forms of experimental colleges, inside of, although quarantined from the existing system (SDS pamphlet).

It is wrong, then, to encourage kids to drop out of public schools. If kids stay in school, the argument goes, they will have to develop forms of political struggle just to survive. Whereas if they leave they will never become politically conscious. They will turn inward, entering the fantasy world of drugs, astrology, and eastern mysticism. Many movement "heavies" distrust the "feelies" among the young. I, too, was disturbed by the changes that some of the kids had undergone since they had left the public schools. Jeremiah, who was a keen social activist when he was at Blair, had become a mystic who felt that verbal communication hindered understanding. At Blair we had been quite close to each other, but now we were worlds apart.

My experience in the school taught me that the distinction between "personal" and "political" change was a facile one, that structural change would be hollow unless it was accompanied by a transformation in consciousness, in the quality of social relationships. Like other counterinstitutions—free clinics, food co-ops, underground papers—free schools develop human needs—of self-determination, communality, spontaneity—that capitalism suppresses in its pursuit of greater efficiency, greater profit. Our project was helping us to unlearn the habits that growing up in our society and years of schooling had ingrained in us.

1. Public Schools: The Education of Future Workers

The schools we went to had tried to make us into disciplined workers who could function in highly bureaucratized organizations. (I use the term "workers" to mean people in jobs—whether as assembly-line workers or teachers—who have little or no control over the conditions or goals of their work.) Bureaucracies—whether in the corporations, the research laboratories, the hospitals, the trade unions—have a hierarchical structure. The top administrators make the basic policy decisions or guidelines, and these rules are passed down the chain of command. Workers in these organizations, however technically skilled, must perform specialized tasks in a plan that they had no share in determining. Organizations do a more predictable job, are more productive and profitable, when the decision-making process runs most smoothly.

Students must learn to accept their own impotence as an inevitable fact of life. What better preparation for the work world is there than studying in an institution where your day is managed for you, where you have no power over what you are taught or how, and no control over what interests your school serves? The "best," the most pliable students, are the ones who have learned to distrust their own instincts. In the place of their own feelings they internalize the apparently "objective" demands of the public school authorities. In their future jobs they will work for material rewards, just as they now compete for grades, the approval of their peers, parents, and teachers. Jules Henry, in *Culture Against Man* makes this point very well:

> In a society where competition for the basic cultural goods is a pivot of action, people cannot be taught to love one another, for those who do cannot compete with one another, except in play. It thus becomes necessary for the school to teach children how to hate, without appearing to do so, for our culture cannot tolerate the idea that babes should hate each other. How does the school accomplish this ambiguity? Obviously through competition itself, for what has greater potential for creating hostility than competition?

Good workers also make good consumers. Fun makes up for the boring routine the student goes through every day. Unable to enjoy himself at his work, he can at least buy one of the many products available in the "teen-age market." Passive in the classroom, he is a perfect victim for advertising in the marketplace. Since our society does not allow him real self-reliance, he must depend on his parents for cash. How else can he sate his appetite for the latest rock records or mod clothes?

It is his constant subjection to authority he does not control that shapes the personality of the student. One encounter with a teacher who hassles him for being out of class is a much more effective lesson than a hundred classes. The world students live in is a perfect microcosm of the workplace they are preparing to enter—where being pushed around is just part of the daily routine. Edgar Friedenberg, in his book *The Dignity of Youth and Other Atavisms,* shows a keen understanding of the role that petty harassment plays in colonizing youth:

> Trivial regulation is more damaging to one's sense of one's own dignity, and to the belief, essential to any democracy, that one *does* have inalienable rights, than gross regulation is. The real function of petty regulations like these is to convince youth that it has no rights at all that anybody is obligated to respect, even trivial ones. And this, after all, is what many—I think—most Americans believe.

And if a student doesn't appreciate his "training"—if he wants to drop out of school—he has to face the sanctions the state has devised to keep him in line. The attendance laws, strengthened by the control that parents exercise over their children (in Maryland, even though a student is sixteen he still needs his parents' permission to withdraw from school), keep kids in school, where they will be trained to take up available positions in the labor market. The destruction of basic liberties, which Friedenberg discusses in the following passage, is no accident—it is a necessary consequence of the role schools play in disciplining future workers:

> . . . our laws governing school attendance do not deal with education. They are not *licensing* laws, requiring attendance until a certain defined minimum competence, presumed essential for adult life, has been demonstrated. They are not *contractual;* they offer no remedy for failure of the school to provide services of a minimum quality. A juvenile may not legally withdraw from school even if he can establish that it is sub-standard or that he is being ill-treated there. If he does, as many do, for just these reasons he becomes *prima facie* an offender; for, in cold fact, the compulsory attendance law guarantees him nothing, not even the services of qualified teachers. It merely defines, in terms of age

alone, a particular group as subject to legal restrictions not applicable to other persons.

The curriculum also helps to produce the narrowly specialized citizen who is prepared to play his appointed role in the social division of labor. John Holt, in *How Children Fail*, discusses the assumptions that inform much of public school teaching:

> Behind much of what we do in school lie some ideas, that could be expressed roughly as follows: (1) of the vast body of knowledge there are certain bits and pieces that can be called essential, that everyone should know; (2) the extent to which a person can be considered educated, qualified to live intelligently in today's world and be a useful member of society, depends on the amount of this essential knowledge that he carries about with him; (3) it is the duty of schools, therefore, to get as much of this essential knowledge as possible into the minds of children.

This analysis needs to be expanded. Students only get "bits and pieces" of information, because the fragmentation of knowledge helps to create obedient workers. The larger and more integrated a perspective one has on the technological process, the more discontented one will become with a subordinate position, with only being a cog in the machine.

Thus the student learns science independently from an investigation of the political economy. He studies how an automobile engine works but doesn't learn why corporations have taken so long to develop a pollution-free engine. He does not have to ask himself about what interests his research will serve, who will fund it, and what social priorities will guide his work. He takes a government course that emphasizes the importance of electoral politics, the legislative process, and pressure groups, but says little about the massive impact of corporate power on the political system. In order for students to accept their training the schools must conceal the fact that the education they are providing has an ideological purpose. Students must believe that they are acquiring empirical, thoroughly neutral knowledge.

2. Survival and Political Consciousness

As we create projects that embody new values we will have to carve out a space for ourselves and protect it against the harassment policies of the state. Even though they have left the custody of the public schools, kids in free schools will still have to deal with other institutions and laws that limit their freedom. There are just no secure islands to escape to.

Labor laws prevent them from holding many jobs if they are under eighteen. Young people frequently cannot rent apartments unless an "adult" is willing to take responsibility for them, to sign the lease in their behalf. Curfews and antiloitering laws restrict their freedom of movement and give police the incentive to abuse them—to search them, to conduct "investigative arrests," to ask them to "move on" from places where they aren't wanted. The drug laws are yet another weapon the state can use to keep the young in a state of fear while suppressing a vital ingredient of their culture.

The police, health, and fire departments harass communes. Many cities have laws that check the growth of communes by restricting their occupancy to no more than four or five persons unrelated by blood, marriage, or legal adoption. Judge Albert C. Wallenberg of the U.S. District Court of northern California in a recent decision provides the rationale for this definition of the "family":

> There is a long recognized value in the traditional family relationship which does not attach to the "voluntary family." The traditional family is an institution reinforced by biological and legal ties which are difficult or impossible to sunder. It plays a role in educating and nourishing the young which far from being voluntary is often compulsory. . . . The communal living groups represented by the plaintiffs share few of the above characteristics. They are voluntary, with fluctuating memberships who have no legal obligation of support or cohabitation. They are in no way subject to the state's vast body of domestic relations law. They do not have the biological links which characterize most

families (quoted in Albert Solnit, "Wear and Tear in the Communes," *Nation*, April 26, 1971).

The young have few civil liberties, few rights that they can use to protect themselves from injuries done them by their parents, the schools, the police. The juvenile courts have traditionally acted in ways that reinforce the control that parents have over their children. Montgomery County Circuit Court Judge John Moore in a decision (Maryland *vs.* Gouge) challenging the practices of the juvenile court describes how this institution has robbed young people of their rights:

> The traditional theory of the juvenile court is that it is primarily a social agency whose purpose is to treat and rehabilitate children rather than determine their guilt or innocence. A finding of delinquency may be based on a preponderance of evidence rather than beyond a reasonable doubt. The public is generally excluded from the proceedings and no transcript is made. The strict rules of evidence are not followed. The constitutional protections traditionally available to the accused criminal do not exist. There is no jury. Representation by counsel is not frequent. These characteristics may be summed up in the term "parens patriae" which has been traditionally employed to denote the doctrinal basis for such procedure. The term contemplates that neglected dependent and delinquent children be made wards of the state which shall exercise the necessary discipline and guardianship when it is lacking in the home.

Any counterinstitution, then, that creates new kinds of social relationships threatens powerful interests. The University of California at Berkeley, for example, had to destroy People's Park because the park was a spontaneous creation that was managed by the people who built it. The students put up a tremendous struggle to save their turf, to defend it against the Berkeley and Alameda County police.

The university administrators could not imagine a use of space that was not subject to bureaucratic criteria. As Sheldon Wolin and John Schaar put it:

> The occupants of the Park wanted to use the land for a variety of projects, strange but deeply natural, which defied customary

forms and expectations, whereas, at worst, the University saw the
land as something to be fenced, soil-tested, processed through a
score of experts and a maze of committees, and finally encased in
the tight and tidy form of a rational design. At best, the most
imaginative use of the land the University could contemplate was
a "field experiment station" where faculty and graduate students
could observe their fellow students coping with their environment (*New York Review of Books,* June 19, 1969).

The struggle over People's Park was definitely a watershed
in the development of the movement. Young people were fighting in their own behalf to protect something they had *created*
and *needed* rather than for some distant, abstract cause. The
political consciousness of people involved in counterinstitutions is born as they try to survive against very difficult odds.
Let me illustrate this point with an account of Freedom
House, a project in Bethesda, Maryland, and of our experiences in a free-school commune.

Freedom House was a rundown, three-room bungalow, located in Bethesda, Maryland, a wealthy suburb of Washington. It was next to the Bethesda Surf Shop, which was frequented by kids hostile to Freedom House, and nine blocks
away from the city's police headquarters. Brint Dillingham, a
former probation officer in Montgomery County, rented the
house in 1968 for Compeers Inc., an organization of which he
was executive director. Compeers had begun as a human-
relations group, as an effort to break down barriers between
suburban and inner-city youth through seminars, tutorials,
and cultural activities. Under Brint's leadership it began programs that spoke to the special needs of white suburban high
school kids.

The original conception of Freedom House was that it
would be a place that would offer services to kids that were
unavailable elsewhere—draft counseling, legal aid, a printing
press for high school underground papers. It was a center for
grape boycott activities and a headquarters for the Student Alliance, a group working for the reform of the Montgomery
County schools. But it soon developed into a kind of "liber-
ated zone," a place where kids who felt uncomfortable most

everywhere else could gather. It was a much better place to be than Hot Shoppes, McDonald's or the bars and discothèques that catered to a teenybopper crowd. Most important it was their own house. Kids came there to see friends, listen to music, do dope, or to "crash" for a night.

As Freedom House developed in this direction the Student Alliance decided to move its office out. A number of people in the student group felt that the kids hanging around the house were "irresponsible." The Freedom House regulars felt that the Alliance was a staid and conservative organization. The Alliance, they felt, had too much faith in the goodwill of the school administration; it had spent too much time working through the established channels. The Alliance had been circulating its report on the Montgomery County school system and had been trying to initiate a dialogue with the school board and the county administrators.

The police soon began a campaign to harass the kids at Freedom House. They put it under surveillance. Police in marked and unmarked cars watched it, shined their headlight beams into the house, took down license-plate numbers, and sometimes followed kids who frequented it. Once the kids caught a plainclothes cop hiding in the bushes outside the house. The police felt free to enter and search it without a warrant. When one of the kids asked a cop if it was legal to do this, he replied: "We are not searching, we are just looking. We don't need a search warrant because we are only looking." On March 12, 1969, the police came into the house to arrest an alleged runaway but presented no arrest or search warrant.

Montgomery County Circuit Court Judge James Pugh on March 3 had asked a grand jury to investigate the *Washington Free Press* for possible subversive activities. Since a number of people at Freedom House sold the underground paper in the county, the police were even more suspicious of activities going on there. On March 20 the police detained two kids from the house who were selling the *Free Press* for "routine investigation." Soon thereafter police arrested Brint Dillingham and a seventeen-year-old kid, who were selling the newspaper across from the Bethesda police station, on the grounds of possessing obscene literature. Brint had decided to test the county's right to interfere with the rights of free press. The *Free Press* issue had a five-page article criticizing Judge Pugh and a cartoon of the naked judge masturbating before the bench. When he came to trial Judge Pugh sentenced Dillingham to six months and set a $5,000 bond for his release. (A year later the court of appeals overturned Brint's conviction.)

Dillingham's arrest triggered a protest by about fifty kids, who marched from Freedom House to a Montgomery County Council meeting to demand that it hear their case against police harassment. The council reacted to their arrival with real paranoia. Here is the *Washington Post* account (April 18, 1969) of the precautions the council took to protect itself against the "invaders":

> Ashtrays were removed from Montgomery County Council chambers in Rockville yesterday because "they might be used as weapons." "No smoking" signs were put there because there were no ashtrays.
> Potted plastic plants and pictures were removed from the hall outside to assure they wouldn't be trampled in a melee.
> Then last night helmeted police and detectives—at least 30 in number—gathered with their cameras outside the Council chambers.

A month later the council allowed Freedom House representatives to testify about the abuse they had suffered from the Bethesda police. In the end, though, the council refused to put the police under any effective control. One of the councilmen, Republican James Gleason, saw in the young people's charges nothing more than a revolutionary plot to subvert established authority: "I am concerned with attempts to bring public disaffection with police all over the country. They usually make charges of harassment and then ask for a public answer. I don't intend to give aid to that movement. . . . We are faced with revolutionary minds, whose purpose is certainly not law and order" (Montgomery County *Sentinel*, May 22, 1969).

The final confrontation between the police and the people of Freedom House grew out of a dispute over the use of the county garage opposite the house. One of the kids involved in

Freedom House had sprayed the heads of 179 parking meters in the garage with black paint. Political slogans—such as "Revolt for Peace"—were written on the walls. On the basis of this incident the police began to prevent kids they suspected of being connected with Freedom House from using the garage. Some kids claimed that the cops threatened to arrest them if they tried to park there.

Other kids in the area heard about the conflict and began coming to Freedom House to take part in the action. By Friday night of that tense week, there were about 100 kids gathered around the house, facing police determined to prevent them from using the garage. They provoked each other. The cops arrested 16 kids that night on charges of disorderly conduct and obstructing traffic.

Soon thereafter they received a notice of eviction from the house. An acquiescent council had permitted the police to win a victory. But Dillingham and many of the high school kids he mobilized continued to organize against the practices of the juvenile courts, the police, and other county institutions. Brint later ran for Sheriff of Montgomery County.

The struggle over the use of the garage was more a symbolic issue than anything else. It was the logical culmination of the police campaign to destroy the only space in Bethesda that the kids could freely enjoy and control. Like the creators of People's Park, the kids of Freedom House were forging their own life style on their own turf without administrative "supervision." And in the eyes of the state this was sufficient reason for their project to be destroyed.

The police, FBI, school board, housing department, and zoning board badgered our project. Sometimes it seemed as if we spent most of our energy just trying to stay out of the way of the authorities or responding to the latest act of harassment. Consider the amount of time we spent dealing with our housing problems—looking for places to live, negotiating with real estate agents, pacifying landlords. Our experiences taught the kids in the school something that no lecture on politics ever could—that it was not possible to "do your own thing" when doing it rubbed abrasively against the interests of others. Threats to our survival sometimes spurred us to break out of our isolation, to become politically involved in our neighborhood.

After the housing inspector visited our home in Takoma Park we talked with the Appalachian kids in the neighborhood about our fears. They were quite sympathetic to our plight; they had been hassled by the Takoma police for walking around late at night, for violating the regulations on the use of motor bikes, and for other petty things. They also had an instinctive distrust of authority. They had moved around a lot and probably identified with our transient existence. One of the younger boys had been in and out of reform school and had recently moved with his mother from Alabama.

We also learned some very interesting things from our Danish landlady, which helped give us some perspective on the housing official's visit. The land our home was on, she said, was very valuable property, which a real estate speculator could easily exploit. A man who lived nearby had been pressuring her to sell it to him. She thought that he wanted to build a shopping center on the land surrounding the house (another woman we were in contact with guessed that he planned to build garden apartments). It was a superb location for a shopping center, since it sat directly above the Maple Avenue area, a perfect market to tap. The speculator, she conjectured, had pushed the city to harass her over the last several years.

It was rapidly becoming clear that our own fate was intertwined with the economic development of the Takoma Park-East Silver Spring area. If the city could force us to leave our home, because of the political muscle of real estate speculators, they could do the same to our neighbors. It was in our own interest to prevent the transformation of Takoma Park into a densely packed commercial area, and it was in theirs also. Maybe, I hoped, this fact would help to break down the barriers that existed between us.

Simon and I thought about writing a leaflet that would connect the repression visited on us with the fate of the neighborhood. But to do this effectively we needed to get more evidence to build our case. The acquisition of knowledge never seemed more urgent; what we were learning related directly to our survival. We went over to the city government building and got copies of the statutes and charter of Takoma Park, the minutes of recent City Council meetings, and the proposed building code. Simon got a map of the zoning plan for Montgomery County. Ruby and I pored through the files on Takoma Park history in the library and started going to council meetings. Some of us went over to spend an afternoon with Sammy Abbott, who had led the fight against the freeway.

I became very interested in the politics of suburban planning, in how decisions were made to promote the expansion of shopping centers, high-rises, highways. I began to ask myself whose interests suburban development served and who paid for the expenses involved in the creation of these projects. How did the growth of shopping centers and high-rises affect land costs and the tax load on working people, whose incomes were already being squeezed by an inflationary economy?

We invited our legal adviser, Stan Sloss, over to the house one evening to discuss the Takoma Park and Montgomery County housing code with members of the school. We learned about the distinction between a "single-family dwelling" and a "rooming house." We began to plot the legal steps we could use to forestall eviction. If all else failed, Steve, Simon, and I planned to stay in the house and force the police to take us out bodily.

We tended to work best when we were confronted with an immediate crisis. But when the threat to our survival was no longer apparent, it was easy to return to our normal behavior. This is what happened to our research on the zoning issue. We started work on it with a flurry of activity, but when it no longer looked as though we would be evicted, our energies began to dissipate. We also did not have a long-range strategy to help us connect our own condition with that of our neighbors. I suspect that this was due to our transient life style, itself a product of our class origins. We did not see ourselves rooted in this community, and our neighbors did. We all had plans to travel and work in other places. Takoma Park was just one stop on our journey.

When the police began harassing us in the early fall we decided it would be best to ignore them. We had learned a great deal from the Freedom House experience about police strategy —that the cops were obviously out to taunt us, to make us so mad that we would get in an argument or scuffle with them. We decided to put our energies into forming a community group, so that we would have a buffer between us and the city. Evan and I worked with a couple from Takoma Park to set up a meeting of adults who would be sympathetic to our cause.

Steve and Evan became involved with the Takoma Park Community Action Forum, a politically moderate organization that was setting up public meetings on issues that affected the community. One night in October a group of us went to a town meeting, "All Together for an Altogether Safe Community," sponsored by the forum. I began to work with some women in the area who wanted to start a community newspaper. I also tried to interest people in the school in the idea of starting a printshop. But both the women and I were overextended in our activities and our project never got off the ground. When the police stopped bothering us we again lost much of our enthusiasm for practical organization in the community.

Our hassles with city laws and agencies were compounded by the fact that we lived in neighborhoods where our presence was resented. We were perfect victims for repression, because we could not rely on our neighbors for support. In Mount Pleasant our "hippie" house stuck out like a sore thumb. We were an island of freaks in a community where many people aspired to break out of the cycle of ghetto life. Our extravagant appearance, the life style of voluntary poverty we had adopted, mocked the values of social mobility that our neighbors believed in.

Communal living was a luxury they couldn't afford. We could always leave Mount Pleasant; they were trapped. We became targets for kids who wanted to hustle us, who came to visit us only to take watches, records, money—the symbols of our middle-class background. Some of the kids in the school felt that it was possible to break down the barriers between us and the people in the neighborhood. They wanted the black kids to trust us. I am skeptical that dialogue, acts of philanthropy, would have brought us closer together. In fact, a conscious attempt to win our neighbors' friendship might have made them distrust us even more. A chasm of class and racial antagonism separated us from each other.

We also clashed with the white working-class people who lived near us in Takoma Park. Our involvement with the kids in the neighborhood had been phony to begin with. We welcomed them in the house whenever they wanted to come in and set standards for them different from those we set for ourselves. If they were making too much noise or were getting in our way we were reluctant to tell them so. We rarely talked with them about our backgrounds, our reasons for having started the school, for living in the neighborhood.

They must have sensed that our life style was shot through with contradictions—our attitudes toward property and theirs were worlds apart. We were living a shabby existence but always had several fancy cars parked outside the house. We owned property we didn't take care of. We left the door of the house open and our rooms were never locked. They were poor and envied the material possessions we were so casual about. Since it was clear to them that we didn't care about property, they decided to see if they could get away with stealing some of our money.

City laws also exacerbated already tense relationships between young and old people in the commune. Some of the sharpest conflicts we had were a direct result of the city's restrictive housing ordinance—which did not permit young people to sign their own leases. Since the older people living in the houses had to sign the leases, we assumed legal responsibility for everything that went on there. We told kids that the house was "their place," that they could make the basic decisions about the living situation. But our words never really rang true. For if they made the "wrong decision" we would have to pay the price for their mistakes—we would be guilty of "contributing to the delinquency of minors," of "maintaining a disorderly house." The law had made us into cops and guardians of public morality.

Despite our trials, the school met certain tangible tests of survival. We maintained three communes and one "community center" (the house in Silver Spring) the second year. But we never tackled the most urgent task of all—the creation of a financially self-sufficient community. Since funds from parents and the foundation grant were easy to come by, we didn't have to search for a way to support ourselves. If the demands on our survival had been greater, we would have had fewer identity crises, our communes would have been much less incestuous. Free schools will naturally find their direction once they start struggling for self-reliance.

A close friend of mine, Larry Aaronson, a former Montgomery County teacher, has suggested that free school and high school students create self-supporting projects—cooperative radio stations, garages, leathercraft shops, printing presses. Here they would acquire skills while generating capital to support themselves. Most important of all, these institutions would be *their own*—cooperatively managed and controlled. And kids would have a real incentive to protect themselves if the authorities tried to close their projects down.

Free schools might serve the kids working in these ventures by providing them with the perspective and knowledge they need for their practical work. A kid working in a free clinic might study biological sciences and medical skills as well as the political and economic framework in which organized medicine operates. As free schools become clusters of self-help projects, study groups built around the acquisition of useful knowledge would take the place of "classes."

Skills centers can also help to break down the artificial separation between "mechanical" and "verbal" knowledge that is fundamental to the public school curriculum. Since middle-class kids are tracked into college prep courses, they graduate from school ignorant and often contemptuous of manual labor. The curriculum thereby strengthens the barriers that divide working-class kids—sequestered in shop courses—from the sons and daughters of professionals. As they learn electronics and mechanics, middle-class kids may discover common ground with students they once had scorned as "greasers."

If the adults in the school had been involved in projects that supported us and really utilized our skills, we would have been more authentic instructors. If I had been working in a print-shop that put out a paper in Takoma Park and that published radical research on the suburbs, I would have been able to offer more to people in the school. In fact, some of the best teachers we had were people who spent much of their day doing their own work. For example, Marc Sommer was writing his autobiography; Ira Levine has skills in printing, silk-screening, and mechanics; and Karl Hess was doing metal sculpture when he wasn't writing or trying to organize a libertarian movement against the state.

Until the organizers of free schools are engaged in both intellectual and practical activity, we will not be able to create radical alternatives to the public schools. The men and women who created revolutionary universities, Staughton Lynd points out (*Intellectuals, the University, and the Movement,* New England Free Press pamphlet), overcame the limitations that set us back: "There is no getting away from the fact that universities combining theory and practice, like the University of Havana whose students work together in the cane fields, or the University of Yenan where students grew their own food, wove their own clothes, and graduated together to fight the Japanese, can only be created by individuals who combine theory and practice personally."

Like many free schools, we still accepted the assumptions of traditional learning theory which divides knowledge into "theoretical" and "practical" fields. But true knowledge, as Mao Tse-tung argues in his lecture *On Practice,* comes from active engagement with social reality:

> If you want to know a certain thing or a certain class of things directly, you must personally participate in the practical struggle to change reality, to change that thing or class of things, for only thus can you come into contact with them as phenomena; only

through personal participation in the practical struggle to change reality can you uncover the essence of that thing or class of things and comprehend them . . .

If you want to know the taste of a pear, you must change the pear by eating it yourself. If you want to know the structure and properties of the atom, you must make physical and chemical experiments to change the state of the atom. If you want to know the theory and method of revolution, you must take part in revolution (*On Practice,* Foreign Languages Press, Peking).

Julius Nyerere, the Prime Minister of Tanzania, envisions a society in which the boundaries between education and material production dissolve. He wants the educational system of Tanzania, a socialist nation, to reflect the cooperative values of agricultural life:

Schools must, in fact, become communities—and communities which practice the concept of self-reliance. The teachers, workers, and pupils together must become the members of a social unit in the same way as parents, relatives, and children are the social unit . . . This means that all schools, but especially secondary schools and all other forms of higher education, must contribute to their own upkeep; they must be economic communities as well as social and educational communities. Each school should have, as an integral part of it, a farm or workshop which provides the food eaten by the community and makes some contribution to the national income.

The school farms must be created by the school community clearing their own bush—and so on—but doing it together. They must be used with no more capital assistance than is available to an ordinary, established, cooperative farm where the work can be supervised. By such means the students can learn the advantages of cooperative endeavor, even when outside capital is not available in any significant quantities. Again, the advantages of cooperation could be studied in the classroom, as well as being demonstrated on the farm ("Education for Self-Reliance," speech).

One of the main tasks of the radical education movement in the next several years should be to reshape Nyerere's vision so it corresponds to the needs of advanced technological society.

3. Back into the System

Building free schools and organizing insurgent movements in mainstream institutions are not contradictory forms of activity, as some have charged. Together they hasten the demise of a school system that is already collapsing. Fred Gardner's response to those who criticize desertion in the army could well be applied to the critics of free schools:

> Judging from the history of how armies fall, it appears that disintegration, not dissent, may characterize the final crisis. There has never been an army that fell apart through the exercise of civil liberties, but there have been some big ones that cracked by mass desertion. As a tactic, desertion has the underrated virtue of simplicity. It is the archetypal anti-war act.
>
> We should not think of desertion mechanically as an alternative to on-base organizing; that's like saying the forehand is alternative to the back hand and therefore a tennis player should only rely on one. The fact is, desertion and dissent are two aspects of the same movement and reinforce one another.

But free schools are more than just a tactic to achieve social change. They also may equip us with the strength and staying power we need to re-enter the system and confront it. When I taught at Blair my fears of failure, my insecurity about losing my job, often immobilized me. I was not confident enough in myself to take real risks.

Living in the school community, sharing in building a project, helped me to discover sources of strength in myself. I became a less private person—more accustomed to collective styles of work and living. As I learned to trust my instincts I found it easier to express my feelings—to risk being vulnerable. Instead of spending my energy doing end runs around a hostile administration, I was beginning to meet my own needs —to chart my own course. But after two years I was weary of the intensity of communal living, of the responsibilities of running a project. I decided to leave the school in the spring of 1970 to find a job teaching in a community college.

I discovered how much the free school had changed me when I began teaching a writing course at Staten Island Community College the following fall. I found that I was capable of doing things that I never could have done at Blair. I spoke out at faculty meetings, made demands on my colleagues, confronted members of the administration. I was less afraid of taking risks, of being fired, because I was not committed to an academic career. Leaving the school system to organize our project had made me less timid, less wary of making fundamental changes in my life.

But I was drawing on emotional resources built up in the past—there was little in my present job or life style that reinforced what I had learned. My experience in our free school sharpened my awareness of the limitations of my job, of the emptiness of my life as a "radical professional."

I was living a schizophrenic existence. I talked of "community," of "collectivity," but my life style betrayed the phoniness of my rhetoric. I lived alone in a small house on Staten Island and shared little with most of my colleagues, who insisted on separating their "private" from their "public" lives. Most New Yorkers I met seemed similarly guarded—afraid of opening themselves up to anybody but their most limited circle. I worked as a lone teacher in a program where we rarely tried to make collective decisions. My students commuted to school from working-class neighborhoods on Staten Island, in Brooklyn, the Bronx, and Queens; our lives only rarely intersected.

I was amazed at how few New York radicals had made any substantial break with their careers. The "heaviness" of their rhetoric, I began to suspect, was a way of compensating for the barrenness of their existence—for still being tied to private households, their jobs, the consumer treadmill. Their politics did not develop organically from their own life styles—it was vicarious. Rather than confront their own frailties—the sources of their own oppression—they looked to workers, blacks, Third World people, or to some other *deus ex machina,* as the vanguard of an American revolution.

As I grew more frustrated with my life style I became more

discontented with my role as a teacher. How, I asked myself, could I discuss ideas in the classroom which my passive condition prevented me from putting into practice? And my students were even more crippled than I was—most of them lived at home dependent on their parents.

One writing class—a discussion of the Vietnam war—crystallized all the doubts I had come to have about my work. We had been analyzing the roots of American intervention in Indochina for the past month. Steve, who was in New York for a few days, was sitting in. Now we were trying to figure out why we found it so hard to resist a war we all agreed was monstrous. Steve, who came from the background much like my students, asked them: "Why do we say that all politicians are crooks and still listen attentively to them on the media?" This was another way of asking why we rarely followed our own best instincts.

Steve was trying to get the kids to relate their political impotence to their dependency on their parents. How, he asked them, can you take political risks when your parents don't allow you any initiative at home—"when your parents always put the milk on the table?" Steve had struck a responsive chord. My students were beginning to understand how trapped they were by the consumer ethic—by a passive orientation to everything around them.

I relearned a lesson that day that my experience in our school had taught me—that rational discussion, that formal classes, which did not occur in a context where people were developing self-reliance, would never change behavior. How useful was it to analyze the Vietnam war when our respective life styles limited our capacity to act together to resist it?

Teaching in a community college made me realize how thoroughly my free-school experience had shaped my consciousness. I discovered how apt a simile Charlie's image of our project was. Living in our school community was like being immersed in a "crucible" that was melting away the chains that bound us to our pasts.

Epilogue

Simon on what he learned at the school:

Contact with people in a high-energy flow—aging at least five years.

Learned a lot of music.

Learned a lot about people.

Learned about Washington community and interrelationships between organizations.

Methods of keeping a structure organic and flexible with age.

How to handle power conflicts in groups.

The evils of money.

How to share.

How not to impose my moral standards on anyone.

How to get stoned with people.

How to "put on" news media.

For many the school was a catalyst that exploded their previous lives and made it nearly impossible for them to return to old-style relationships. Several kids have gone to college, though few have stayed. An exception is Judy, who has been attending college in New England for the past two years. Others have found that college has not satisfied their restlessness, has not helped them learn what they need to know.

Some have set out to learn specific skills: Simon and Cookie are married—he is learning carpentry in a union apprenticeship program; Greg has learned to make dulcimers and other musical instruments; Dave studied drama at college for a year and has done street theater in Berkeley; Norman has founded the Out of the Ashes Press in Portland, which has published his novel, *No Title;* Graham has continued to study music in Baltimore.

Two of the older people who left our project, Ira and Richard, have taken jobs at more structured progressive schools. Joel spent a year teaching at Staten Island Community College and is heading west to find a place to settle. Steve is farming in Pennsylvania. Evan and Carol spent a year at a rural commune in New England and are trying to save money to buy some land of their own. Jeremiah lived on a farm in Costa Rica for several months and learned to farm under extraordinary conditions. Randy is in India, a disciple of the Maharishi.

The school continued as a day school this past year. The people whom we spoke with complained of dispersion and lack of focus. Toward the end of the year we learned the school was considering moving to a farm in Virginia. Perhaps the school (which is a name more than an institution) will be reborn once again with a new set of people and new goals.

STEVE BHAERMAN
JOEL DENKER
June 1971